What Color is Your Medicine?

Author
Dropped
Off
Local Woman

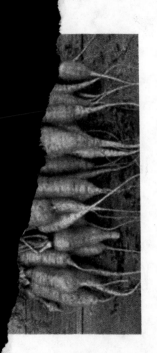

image001.jpg
83K

[Quoted text hidden]

What Color is Your Medicine?

*—Enter the depths of your heart with
the 5 Elements of Chinese Medicine*

by

Regina Powers

Library of Congress Control Number: 2018903967

Paperback ISBN: 9781732195509
1st edition, September 2018
Printed in the United States of America

Cover concept: Regina Powers
Cover art & chapter illustrations: Mickenzie Smith
Layout and production: Kara Adanalian
Back cover photo: Green Nickel photo

Visit SolJourneys.com for more information on the author and her offerings.

This book is dedicated to my parents.

Table of Contents

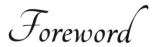 Foreword

by Dr. James E. Lemire

Board-Certified American Board of Family Practice
Student of Master Yun Xiang Tseng for eleven years

IT IS MY PRIVILEGE to write the Foreword of this new book by Regina Powers, a Western-trained practitioner who now utilizes the 5 Elements of Chinese medicine to help patients understand the underlying cause of their disease and use ancient remedies to help improve their health and being.

Regina writes with passion and enthusiasm about her personal journey to health, where she "learned the true art of medicine," and discovered how to rebuild her Qi (Life Energy) and restore her health.

She takes us along on her journey from traditional medicine training into the new field of energy medicine, where she learns the wisdom of Traditional Chinese medicine, which has been well-established for centuries.

The 5 Elements have become a guide for Regina to bring in all parts of a person, as is required for healing to their "truest form." We cannot separate our spirit from our body and achieve wholeness.

Regina presents the 5 Elements with definitions for each: fire, earth, metal, water, and wood. She connects one chapter expertly with the next and uses interesting clinical stories to help define each element. She keeps readers involved with her interesting stories.

She summarizes her book with a Gaelic saying, "Cead Mile Failte" which means "100 thousand welcomes," or "you are welcome, a thousand times, wherever you come from, whoever you are." This is when we finally come home to our body, mind, and spirit, living without separation; truly come home to a heart that is in direct resonance with the energy of yes, where all manifestation flows.

Regina has given us the tools to see all the colors that surround us and how to interpret them through Traditional Chinese Medicine (TCM).

Finally, Regina has come up with some recommendations to open each of the elements that provide an outstanding springboard to improve our lives.

Thank you, Regina. This is an outstanding book with a clear road map for practical ways of healing, using many powerful techniques along with the 5 Elements of Traditional Chinese Medicine.

Blessings,
Dr. James E. Lemire, MD, FAAFP, IFMCP

Thank You...

... to my mother and father, first and foremost. Dad, I know that you have had a hand in so much since your passing. I love you. Mom, you are a true gift of presence. My love for you extends beyond this lifetime. I am so grateful to have you in my life! And of course, to the entire POWERS clan and all its extensions—thank you for a continued lifetime of lessons—ones that keep on giving.

... to the many people I have had the privilege and honor of assisting on their journey. I have sat with so many individuals, families, young and old alike, each a teacher to me. I am grateful to have been a witness into the window of your souls—a gift that allowed me deeper into mine.

...my dearest friend, Jennifer. The wonder and essence of this world are so much brighter with you in it. We have shared many tears, along with abounding fits of laughter, which only living in the present moment can bring. I am very grateful to be trekking along this lifetime with you. I love you, my dear friend.

... to an amazing woman who has been journeying with me for many years, and throughout this entire process, with unwavering support and friendship—thank you, Natalina. Also, my deep gratitude to the many teachers, classmates, and mentors, both Western and Eastern-trained, who are too numerous to thank individually.

...to the Emergency department friends and staff at both MGH-Mass General and BI-Beth Israel Deaconess hospitals in Boston—the places I started my nurse practitioner career. I gained an incredible skill set and it was in my residencies with you that I began to truly see and understand the workings of the human body.

Thank you all!

Introduction

*I*T WAS 1995 and I had just learned that my ex-husband had passed away. I was lying on a table, sobbing, unable to breathe, with a French-speaking healer squeezing my toes. I can recall that day as if it were yesterday—that day changed the course of my life and my life's work. I did not know what it all meant in the larger picture of my life, but on that day, I had my first introduction to the 5 Elements of Traditional Chinese medicine (TCM) and began my journey into energy medicine.

I started with Western medical training, then came the understanding of TCM and specifically the 5 Elements (Earth, Metal, Water, Wood, and Fire). In discovering the wisdom of what the natural world holds for us by way of the 5 Elements, I realized they are, in part, a mirror for us to uncover various holdings within our physical and emotional body, mind, and spirit. I recognized then that the 5 Elements within the natural world—as well as other teachings—had been speaking to me my entire life. I was just learning how to listen.

This book started to write itself. It began to take form in just under two months—it was as if I was being called upon by a force greater than myself, a place within me that longed to be accessed, so I could share the gifts of my soul. We are all connected in one way or another, so I have sprinkled parts of my own journey into these pages. I have included the experiences of other souls for whom I have cared, with the hope that their stories will awaken you and inspire you to find new and different ways to improve your overall health and wellbeing. My intention is that if you wish to learn, heal, and grow, that this book will help you find a deeper meaning in life—and that it will serve as a useful guide you can take with you on your journey.

This book carries healing energy for everyone who chooses to embark on this adventure. If you are looking for ways to heal, if you are hoping to uncover the deeper crevices of your being, may these words speak to you in ways you are ready and willing to hear. On whatever healing path you choose, may you be blessed, and may you become more alive and better equipped to enjoy love, peace, and balance in your everyday life.

The Path of Initiation

MY PATH, like so many people's, took numerous twists and turns in order for me to be right here, right now. Thus far, my journey has delivered no shortages in the lesson department. I believe that all these experiences occurred in order for me to let enough go to come fully into myself. Some people know their calling from an early age. Some dream of being a baker, designer, actor, nurse, or a candy-maker, and on and on it goes. I probably knew from a very young age that I could assist people in some way on their journey of wellness, but to what capacity was pretty much a mystery until now. Our paths in life are rarely straight, and our life's lessons can alter the course of our journeys, bringing us new awareness and new possibilities in the process.

I started out my journey as a nurse's aide in high school, and then went on to nursing school. After becoming a registered nurse, I married my college sweetheart. After ten years together, our marriage ended. Not too long after that, my ex-husband passed away.

It was a horrific loss of a young man in his mid-thirties, a tragedy that became a pivotal point in my life. Those three days during his wake, the funeral, and burial were etched into my entire being—I was utterly numb, every cell of my body was frozen. After the third day, I was driving back to my parents' home and realized I hadn't eaten for those entire three days. I had seen how horrific the experience was for his parents and sister, yet there was nothing I could do or say, other than tell them how sorry I was for their loss.

My ex and I met during my late teens, and we stayed together through my twenties. I had spent a third of my life with him at that point. My mind ran through so many of our stories. In many ways, we grew up together. Then our paths started to change, and we took on different ways of being in the world. I was the one who initiated our breakup—it was something I had to do. Having lived most of my life back east, I relocated to the west coast after our breakup and began to make a new life for myself in California.

After the loss of my ex-husband, my path began to shift when a friend gave me a gift certificate to see a healer. A few months went by, and I had yet to use the gift. After all, I was an avid member of the "I'm fine!" camp and wasn't sure what this healer could do that I couldn't do for myself. My friend called me a few times urging me to see this healer. He kept stressing that the healer might not be in the area for much longer. He normally lived in France and was in the area doing work with the world-renowned surgeon and author, Bernie Siegel. His primary focus of healing was working with the very ill and with people who have had a loss in their life. I listened but didn't really get what all the fuss was about—I had no idea who Bernie Siegel was. I finally made an appointment, without any expectations.

So, off I went, and let's just say my life after this experience was much different than when I walked in to see this person. As I entered his space, I thought, "Well this is a really cool room with a killer view of San Francisco." So, if nothing else, that was nice. I had taken the bus from where I was living to an area of San Francisco called Buena Vista. It was a loft-type apartment, and I could see the treetops through windows which enveloped his healing room. It felt like I was in a jungle tree house and that helped me feel somewhat comfortable.

The healer spoke very few words of English and as I lay down on his healing table, I realized he didn't need me to say much of anything. He knew exactly what was needed. I felt his hand go directly over my heart and the tears instantly started to flow. They never stopped for the entire time I was supine (face-up) on that table. It felt like an eternity…an hour of non-stop tears. I wept and wept so much I couldn't breathe through my nose, so he squeezed my toes. Miraculously, this cleared up my sinuses, and I could once again breathe. I thought, "Wow, what a cool trick!" My time had finished, and he left the room. I got up and sat on his couch. I felt like someone had just wrung me out to dry.

What happened next was like something out of a Sci-Fi movie. Let's just say, that right then I realized that everything I had thought was crazy couldn't compare to my new standard of crazy. Nothing was ever as real for me as it was in that moment. I knew the way in which the world works was a mystery—just as we are a mystery. Our abilities to see, hear, taste, feel, and smell are tangible and palpable. I thought I knew a lot, having studied the workings of the human body. I was comfortable seeing a new life come into the world or being with illness and death. I could stand alongside another person who was going through some of the most trying times in their life.

When the healer came back into the room, I'm sure I looked as if I had seen a ghost. In his thick French accent, he said, "Yes, your beloved is here. He sits beside you. I am so sorry your heart is so sad." Now, mind you, I had not told this man anything. No real conversation had transpired prior to the healing…a mere "Bonjour," as he had welcomed me and showed me where to place my belongings. He then pointed for me to lay on his table. He had no idea I had lost someone, let alone that I had been married to him. Later, I spoke with the friend who had gifted me with the healing, and he confirmed that he had not told the healer anything about me—I had just gone in for a healing, gift certificate in hand.

Before the healer had come back into the room, the room had filled with a very familiar scent. It was my ex-husband—he was with me in that room. We had had a weight room in our home and when he worked out, he emitted a very unique odor, an unmistakable scent. It was not foul, it was just him. Whenever I think about that moment in the healer's room, it all comes back to me instantly, as if it was yesterday. There was no memory of anything—no thoughts of how my relationship didn't work out, no thoughts of when it did. It was his spirit and the opening of mine in our purest form—no blame, no shame, no pointing of fingers. It was an amazing feeling that enveloped my entire being for that brief moment. With my heart wide open, I was able to receive what I understood to be love without conditions—such a rare and precious gift! God bless you, my friend, and thank you.

AFTER THAT HEALING, I got on the bus to make my way home. I remember having two men chat me up, one right after the other. I surmised they were hitting on me. First at the bus stop, then again while standing on the bus, holding onto a handle. Yes, after one hour of a tear fest! *They must be blind*, I thought. *I must look a mess!* Then I walked into my apartment and my roommate asked, "Did you cut your hair? You look great!" I thought, *I'm not really sure what's going on here.* I had not done anything different, other than crying for an hour. The next day at work, I heard the same kind of comments from my co-workers. "Wow, you look great! What did you do?" I tried to make sense of it all...*you cry for an hour and you look better?! What?!*

I realized the amount of emotional stress I had been carrying had been visibly displayed on and in my physical body. This was a bit of a shocker, as there was no mention of this in any of my understandings thus far. I also discovered how good we humans are at storing or hiding our emotions from ourselves and one another.

This experience was what began my knowing of how life's tragic events can remain hidden in our emotional and physical bodies. I guess it would make sense then that illness can make its way into the body if these emotions are not released. I was grateful I had gone to see the healer. We all know that stress affects us but until that healing, I did not know it was visible to the naked eye.

I also did not realize I was doing this "holding thing," because I lived within that "I'm fine!" camp. I did still wonder…were those tears only my unprocessed grief, or did it also have to do with other things yet to be processed from my past? I felt it was likely a combination of the two. I presumed that we must also hold all our other emotions as well, or at least attempt to. Then, I wondered what all this would look like in my body down the road, if these emotions were unexpressed and left to fester.

I did have quite a release that day, because I left feeling physically and emotionally lighter. I could even breathe easier. Since I had cried throughout the entire session, I figured I must still have more of this "holding thing" going on. So, I decided to go back twice more to the healer. Each time I shed less tears than I had the time prior. I had so many questions as I began navigating this path of uncertainty. My interest was piqued, and I was certain there was more to learn. I had only just scratched the surface.

The truth is, in that moment, I had no clue what this thing called "healing" really meant or looked like. I also realized that what occurred in that room would likely stay in that room. I mean, in what type of forum would this be spoken about or taken seriously, especially in the Western medical world? I could never explain this to the medical world I took part in each day…that world that had a nice set of rules and protocols all laid out, a world that was given accolades for living predominantly in their minds. I was quite comfortable in that world, though I had always known there was more to our ways of being, other than living from the neck up. It was one of the reasons I probably overcompensated in the world of medicine, to make up for the fact that I was a lot more comfortable in the world of energy.

AFTER THAT HEALING, I began to test out sharing my thoughts about energy medicine with others. Initially, if I referred to the terms "energy" or "energy medicine," I would sense a shift in the person I was speaking to...a shift displayed by a rolling of the eyes or an abrupt change of subject. I knew that the energy healing I had received penetrated to the depths of my core and touched a place I had yet to experience before then. And, that another person's energy—the energy of a person who had passed—could appear seemed a bit perplexing at the time. I had yet to study about it or understand the language of energy. I think that when you know the truth in the deepest part of your being, no words or language are necessary. Your soul speaks only the language of truth.

We have many layers to us. Our physical layer is only one. I have come to learn that these layers are vast energy fields. Our energy fields include our physical, emotional, intellectual (mind), and spiritual levels, and they extend outward, reaching out into the universe. Many people refer to these levels of energy surrounding the body as an *aura*, or *auric field*. These energetic layers can be seen in a photograph using Kirlian photography. Dr. Barbara Brennan's book, *Hands of Light*, has wonderful, in-depth descriptions and illustrations of these energy levels and fields. *Auric fields* contain a variety of colors that shift and change depending upon multiple factors, such as what you put into your body, or what you're experiencing physically and emotionally.

If we cut off part of a leaf and look at it with Kirlian photography, we can still see the energy field of the entire leaf even though part of the structure is no longer there. This phenomenon is similar to the experience of "phantom pain"—when a person loses a limb or a body part, they may still feel sensations or pain in the area that is gone. In part, the energy field of that body part still exists ... it's still part of the whole physical structure energetically. We do not always see or know what's working for us in the larger picture of the universe, let alone in our daily lives.

Having had the energy of a deceased loved one appear in my energy field at one of the most vulnerable times of my life, showed me new possibilities in the vastness of what exists beyond our "ordinary" lives. If we can remain open to the never-ending magic and mystery of the universe, we may discover that energy medicine may be far more powerful in affecting the overall improvement of our health and well-being than we ever thought possible.

It appears that I was a bit more open to these otherworldly activities than I had thought because I didn't have much trouble digesting what had occurred with this healer. That I chose to keep it to myself was about how I thought others would react. To be honest, this was not the first time I had opened up to the possibility that we are more than our physical bodies, although it was the first time another person had witnessed me opening up. I soon realized that when people are without their defenses in place (like when my heart broke open during that healing), it's as if the truth of what exists—either seen or unseen—can come forward. Then, if we feel safe enough while another person witnesses or acknowledges us, we can have a deeper healing experience. The tears I shed were a normal human response; tears assist us in bringing balance back into our systems. But tears are a gift and in order for us to receive the gift, we have to open up and allow ourselves to release.

IN A STRANGE WAY, that day helped clarify some things for me. The world I thought I knew had little to do with what I had learned thus far in the classroom. I started to awaken, or re-awaken, a part of me that knew intuitively there was more for me to learn and explore in this lifetime. I started to feel some sort of gravitation pull for my soul to awaken. I got a sense of the many masks we use, like trying to hold everything together in that "I'm fine!" camp. This was a part of the defense system I had set strongly in place.

There are so many defenses we can use, and we do this somewhat unconsciously as a way to help us avoid any recall of unpleasant feelings related to traumatic events. "Regression," for example, is one such defense, to protect one's self from re-experiencing the overwhelming feelings of a trauma or event. A person regresses back to a younger age of development or a happier time. Another example is the defense of "denial." Most of us can relate to wanting to avoid or deny recalling an unpleasant feeling or a traumatic event, so we unconsciously deny it. I call the mechanics of these defenses "holding patterns," and over time we can develop many muscles to hold on with. The weight of these defenses is exhausting, as the energy they take can leave us drained, without knowing or understanding why we are doing it. These defenses or holding patterns may then contribute negatively to our overall health, and they can do untold damage—to ourselves and to those around us.

Originally, this path started out as a way to begin my grieving process. But, as I said, I understood that this path was leading me to a place of opening—opening my heart to love and allowing my heart to heal. I could have never imagined that the depth of love transmitted to me that day even existed. That healing allowed me to let enough go in order to make room to receive that gift—a gift that helped me get through one of the most difficult times in my life.

These experiences were the start of my journey of exploring the various ways in which we carry and hold our trauma and emotions within ourselves. We do this to keep ourselves contained and to remain separate from one another. The healing session I had cracked me wide open and demonstrated how this opening brought forth the expression of my true beauty, which was reflected to me by others who shared that with me following the healing. It was obviously not in the way my hair or makeup looked. It was, in fact, the expression of what true beauty was and is, in our purest form. It's been said more than once how the process of letting go can be far more difficult than the act of holding on. Once we let enough go, we can begin to receive and allow more aspects of our truth and innate beauty to come forward. God knows, it takes up far more time, space, and energy for us to hold onto things that sadly can inhibit the natural flow and freedom to and from our precious hearts.

2

What is this thing called "healing" ... really?

A FEW YEARS LATER, well past my healing experience, I was accepted into graduate school, making my way from being a registered nurse to becoming a family nurse practitioner, an advanced practice role which included assessment, diagnosis, and the ability to prescribe medication to treat patients with both acute and chronic illness. A place I was eager to begin.

After I finished graduate school, I moved back east. I started working in the Emergency Department (ED) at one of the major teaching hospitals in Boston. The ED was a familiar place for me, as I had been an ED and trauma nurse for many years. It was full of many physicians, residents, and medical students, which provided me with an instant backup system, lessening my fears in starting this new role. Initially, I presented each case to an attending physician until I gained his or her trust. It was the start of having a new relationship, seeing and treating people. It was as if I had been granted access into deeper parts of another person's being.

My career was underway. It was a new beginning, and I realized the level and weight of responsibility I had chosen to take on—I had a real understanding that I could indeed cause harm to another human being. Each day, when I walked up to the front entrance of the ED, I recited a prayer. It became part of my daily ritual at the start of each shift. "May I fully assess, diagnose, and treat each person I come in contact with this day. May I cause no harm." It's funny, I can't recall a day that I didn't say that prayer. I could sense a deep well of compassion building inside of me. It was an awakening of sorts and as time went on, this feeling increased as I saw and treated more and more people.

Each person was like a puzzle. I understood that they were helping me with parts of my own puzzle. Many times, the person who ended up in front of me reflected an aspect of myself in some way. Sometimes, it was something I needed to learn more about, and magically it would appear. For example, I thought I needed to perform more eye exams, so I could get comfortable using a slit lamp. The slit lamp allows you to examine the eye with magnification lenses and assists with making a thorough diagnosis. The day that thought came to me, I ended up doing three slit lamp exams. This happened a lot. I would have a thought, let it go, and what I needed would come to me. It felt like the universe wanted to stretch me and my understandings in order for me to start using my own intuitive abilities.

I continued making my way, asking a lot of questions and approaching each and every person with a very discerning eye. I noticed every minute detail—the way people walked, sat, held themselves or didn't. I watched the way their feet turned in or out, or were aimlessly dangling without them caring if they ever touched down upon the earth. I noticed the way their bodies held their shape, with respect to their story. I observed the way they took in a breath, along with the quality and tone of their voices. I noticed their reactions to their surroundings, to their spouse, to their kids, and to everything and everyone around them.

Many days in that ED, I had people lying on gurneys in a hallway awaiting an exam or waiting for a room to free up. Others were just screaming obscenities or being belligerent because they wanted to be seen. It was just another day in the ED. Through each patient, each puzzle, I was learning and growing, as the physical and emotional makeup of each individual was on full display for my understanding. All of these observations enabled me to learn and take in the various aspects of what makes up a human being. I started to feel more like a detective as the process got underway.

My focus on Western medicine remained for quite some time before I started to delve into what else was out there. At this point, I was in a world that was so far removed from that healing I had experienced that I never thought the two worlds could meet. I was gaining more insight and understandings into the workings of the human body. This was a means to discover the template with which I saw and interpreted each person.

So, the time came, and the exploration of various healing modalities was underway. I continued working as a nurse practitioner throughout these discoveries, and it became quite apparent to me that there were so many other forms of healing. I remember talking to one of the ED physicians and sharing some of my new insights. She turned, looked at me, and said, "You are now learning the true art of medicine." I never forgot that remark.

One day I was suturing someone in the ED, a part of the job I so enjoyed because I got to sit for a bit—it was an opportunity to catch my breath for a moment during a shift. It also included a chance to connect with a variety of colorful people and personalities on any given day. I was suturing a man who started to share his experiences with Chinese medicine. He shared who the practitioners were in Chinatown who were worth checking out. I listened intently. Not long after this encounter, I found myself in Chinatown with someone looking at my tongue, feeling my pulses, and giving me a bag of herbs and some bark to make a medicinal tea. I was told my Qi was off—Qi meaning energy. Apparently, my energy system was out of balance. I had not been aware of this, nor did I even know if it was true. Yet I kept remembering how my life in the "I'm fine!" camp had affected me, and that I was probably still taking up some residence there. I mean, I was working in such a fast-paced, crazy environment most days that I had no problem believing my Qi was off.

Another day while at work, I was still a bit sick from a lingering flu I'd had for over a week. One of the respiratory therapists with whom I was working shared that she was finishing up her acupuncture training and offered to place some needles in me to help with my symptoms. I didn't hesitate and went supine on a gurney. She pulled the curtain and placed the needles. Not long after she took the needles out I thought, "What did she do? I feel great!" So many experiences and people kept coming to me. I had a deep longing to uncover the truth of what this thing called *"healing"* was. I was so grateful for everything and everyone that came along my path.

I SET OUT for my first Integrative Medicine conference in San Diego, California. The first speaker spoke about the 5 Elements of Chinese medicine. He was an internal medicine physician who was originally from China. He had come to the U.S. to study medicine and had ended up working here, leaving behind his grandfather's teachings as a Traditional Chinese Medicine (TCM) practitioner. When he first started seeing patients, he noticed they kept returning after he treated them. He knew he was missing something, so he closed his practice and headed home to China to learn and apprentice with his grandfather. Eventually he returned to the U.S., with a more finely-tuned skill set. He was now a TCM practitioner with a blended practice, which included internal medicine. I followed him around the entire conference. As he spoke, I knew he was speaking the truth. He had a unique gift, and I felt privileged to meet and dine with him over the course of this five-day conference. I felt like a sponge, taking in his teachings. They rang true to my very core.

Then I found my way to Dr. John Thie, the creator of *Touch for Health*. Touch for Health is a technique that utilizes muscle testing and acupressure points to open and balance the body. It uses metaphors to explain the 5 Elements and helps guide people to the holdings in their bodies. I became even more fascinated with how well nature and these 5 Elements so nicely traversed the body's landscape. Touch for Health incorporates the entire person's body, mind, and spirit.

After taking everything in from these trainings, I was left with many questions about all this "energy stuff." At this point I had already received my certification as a Reiki I and II practitioner and went on to become a Reiki master.

Then I stumbled upon yet another person. He was a nutritionist and medical intuitive. I wasn't sure what he was all about, but I figured I would check him out. I entered an office with walls lined with books. I walked by a shelf and the book, *Hands of Light*, by Barbara Ann Brennan came flying off the shelf and landed at my feet. I picked it up. He looked at me and said, "I'm sure you probably get that you would benefit by looking her up and perhaps studying with her." So, off I went to see what she was all about.

In my discovery, I learned that Barbara Ann Brennan had been a NASA physicist before her study of energy and healing work. Her private healing practice was booked out a year in advance, and she had many physicians requesting her assistance with difficult cases. So again, my interest was piqued. Barbara couldn't keep up with the volume of clients in her practice, so she decided to open a school. At one point, she had three schools. I hadn't read Barbara's book. I just skimmed through it and went to her workshop (which of course was happening the very next weekend). After that workshop, let's just say another amazing experience in the "realm of crazy" happened, which propelled me to study with Barbara and complete her four-year training program. I learned so much at this extraordinary program, and it launched my work as a healer in energy medicine.

Energy is something we all are. In fact, everything that makes up the universe is energy. It is something that can be measured, and yet it can be a bit challenging to fully comprehend. I like this analogy of explaining how we feel energy: Imagine you get on a bus. You sit down next to someone, but then decide to get up and sit elsewhere. The person didn't say or do anything to you, but something didn't *feel* right. Something was off—you couldn't see it, but you could *feel* it. The person's energy or perhaps their vibration just didn't resonate with yours, so you moved. Albert Einstein said it best: "Everything is energy and that's all there is to it, match the frequency of the reality you want, and you cannot help but get that reality. It can be no other way. This is not Philosophy. This is Physics."

We are one big energetic circuit that functions when our systems are in good working order and even when they're not. Just like when our vascular beds are filled and our precious hearts are pumping to facilitate the perfusion of blood to our organs and muscles; all this is happening in order to keep the body and its energy working. In a perfect system, energy flows effortlessly. However, when we accumulate life events, traumas, and all the associated unexpressed emotions, our bodies attempt to find ways to re-create balance in an unbalanced system. After trying everything in hopes that we can continue to avoid feeling where our circuitry has been rerouted (with these accumulated holdings), our systems start to malfunction. Our bodies' self-healing mechanisms get tired. Our bodies let us know...a new symptom or illness starts to appear. We all learn masterful ways to compensate as we move through life. Sometimes it is a matter of survival or staying safe that we continue to ignore our bodies.

It appears that none of us get through life unscathed—some form of trauma or event usually seems to make its way on board. We take on different defenses, belief systems, or habits as a means to compensate. Over time, our body takes on these various holding patterns. We do this unconsciously, it occurs without us even knowing that it's happening. Instead of feeling and allowing our system to release and let go of what has come our way, we take on this new, guarded way of being in the world.

For example, maybe we notice that we have a new fear which

leads us to experience intermittent bouts of anxiety. Or perhaps we have pent-up anger that we never thought was an issue—until we begin to push people away, binge eat, or start to take in one-too-many libations more frequently. We do these things as a way to avoid, cope, or feel safe. In turn, this may lead us to having back problems or stomach issues. If we continue along this path without taking part in discovering why these things are happening, they begin to spill over into our relationships, work, and family life, if it has not already done so.

Many times, we start to conform to the events life brings us without even realizing we are doing it. We change who we are and how we are in the world as a means to fit in, to feel or stay safe. This adaptive behavior can take place at a very early age—it may even develop *in utero*. Our bodies begin to take on certain shapes or characteristics and continue to do so through to our early adulthood. For example, we may develop a twist in our spine, an off-centered face, or difficulty keeping our feet firmly planted on the earth.

These body traits are an example of a Schizoid characterology. Usually this profile develops after a trauma, which occurred at or before birth through the first year of life. The individual perceives that it's not safe to be here on earth. It's as if their body takes on ways to keep them close to the heavens, keeping them from fully rooting in the physical body here on earth. Stephen Johnson, Ph.D. details in his book, *Character Style*, the description of the various characterology styles that can develop and manifest in the body during a person's life. Things start to show up—experiences, traumas, unexpressed desires and emotions—and we continue to accumulate and store them somewhere in our body. If we don't address them over time, the "picture" of us gets a new frame without us ever knowing we were redecorating the house.

In my own life, I was always finding ways to move. You name it, I did it. I was a roller-blader, a mini tri-athlete—no ironman, just sprints. My favorite event was The Lobsterman triathlon in Maine.

I was also a long-distance cyclist. I did Cycle Oregon, a seven-day ride across Oregon, and participated in the AIDS ride, a seven-day ride from San Francisco to LA. After completing the AIDs ride, a couple of friends and I turned around and did it again, adding in a more coastal route. I was also a casual runner, doing a mere twenty-one-miler while living and working on Martha's Vineyard. I know I have been fortunate to do all these things, but let's just say I was a bit of an Energizer Bunny. Yep, I was non-stop! I was also too busy caring for everyone else's aches, pains, and emotional roller coasters to slow down enough to check in with my own system. I was on a non-stop train and had no idea that I had even gotten on board.

I also realized that this was, in part, my medicine. My body functioned quite well, and I often found my way into the woods and onto a trail. I now understand that being in constant motion was the way I chose to avoid the emotions I held within me. I didn't understand how it's necessary for everyone to fully plant down on the earth until I became privy to the "instruction manual." Then, I realized why I had no difficulty noticing everyone else that couldn't touch down upon the earth. By recognizing this inability in others, I was being shown, over and over, my own reflections. It became my quest to fully plant down on this beautiful planet and inhabit my own body. So, I continued to polish my own mirror while assisting others to see their own reflections in theirs.

In order for me to completely heal, I needed to arrive here on earth, fully grounded. It was the only way I would be able to take Gaia in and deeply receive her. I realized that in order for us to receive our greatest gift, we need to transform our deepest wounding. The Earth is indeed my gift—she allows me to help others receive her wisdom and medicine. I also realized I could only digest a little of her at a time, because the "receiving aspect" of my journey was in itself the hidden gem beneath the earth that I had tried to mine for years.

In the beginning of my second year of energy medicine training, I started to see all that I was holding—it was so much more than I had ever imagined. It wasn't until things were brought up in various trainings and healings that I understood the reality of it all. Moving through life at record speed was not going to help me clear my closets of the many holdings I had accumulated. I started to realize that my system could indeed hold a lot. So much so that it was a bit puzzling. I had been around so much trauma and illness my entire life that I never really thought much about it.

As I began to release things, I got flashes of people from many different places and walks of life. I did not remember seeing most of them in this lifetime. It felt like I was seeing things that had occurred way beyond this lifetime. I concluded, "Well, I'm here now, so let's just be here with what's happening and keep on going."

I remember pairing up with someone at a training who had just completed a trauma release workshop. He knew I had worked with trauma for many years, and as part of our work together he offered this technique, which I now know as Eye Movement Desensitization and Reprocessing therapy (EMDR). It started out with some eye movements and not long after, my head was moving repeatedly at a very fast pace. Right, left, right, left—it felt like an eternity, and yet I'm sure it ended up being only about five minutes total. I experienced release after release after release. When we were finished, I had seen in my "mind's eye" well over a thousand people that were ill or maimed in some way. It was crazy how many faces were flashing in front of my visual field. I felt they were all leaving some hidden corner in me, that I had nicely stored them all away, awaiting this release. Afterward, I felt so at peace. I never spoke of it to anyone other than the person who had facilitated it for me.

I understood at that time that most people have this invisible "emotional garbage can" within them—and that our lives provide us with ongoing experiences or *filling stations*. The only way we know the can is full is when it spills out into our physical and/or emotional bodies and starts to speak to us through various symptoms. It became apparent to me that most of us are waiting for a safe space, so we can take the lid off and release the holdings in our container. I was curious as to how and why I was still functioning so well. At the same time, I knew I had a pretty solid constitution, and I paid close attention to the messages in my body when they spoke to me.

I have always been someone who is very present with people. At times, while I listened to their stories or presenting complaints, I noticed that something within them would start to shift. I began to feel (and sometimes even see) where these holdings were in their bodies. Or, my hands would find the holding—without words—it just happened. When I dropped down into my heart and connected from that space with another person, I began to see parts of their deeper, authentic self magically emerge. From this place, it was as if all the other "stuff" would begin to dissipate, as their true self was able to come forward. The bridge between our mind and body is indeed the heart. This is the space where those hidden emotions can release.

I kept thinking that our ability to heal was getting blocked in some way; something was keeping us away from our hearts, the place where much of our healing occurs. Often our pains, either physical or emotional, take up residence somewhere in our body's tissues or organ structures. All of these pent-up emotions and pain are searching to release, so our system can once again flow freely and receive all that the universe has for us. It's almost as if we need a little crack in our system, so we can let the light in and set our spirits free.

WE ALL STRUGGLE to make our way through life. But our attempts to be perfect do not allow anyone in because there isn't an opening or crack in our system they can get through. This, in turn, makes it harder to truly live, if we are not willing to open and drop down into our hearts so that we can heal organically. As Tibetan Buddhist and teacher Pema Chodron wisely says, "When we protect ourselves, so we won't feel pain that protection becomes like armour, like armour that imprisons the softness of the heart."

At the end of my second year of energy medicine training, I chose to leave emergency medicine and move back to California. It was the discovery of what true balance was beginning to feel like in my own body that precipitated the move. I found it difficult to be in an ED environment that kept me moving at lightning speed. The amount of trauma and illness I saw during each shift never really allowed me to completely clear those deeper crevices of my own being.

I realized that I am a very sensitive empath. I found it easier to switch over to working at a slower pace, at my own private healing practice, where I incorporated integrative functional medicine practices into my work. This gave me more time with people and allowed me to see and bring in the TCM Elements in a way that was more digestible for people, as well as for myself. It also provided me with a deeper understanding of the processes we engage in with our bodies, minds, and spirits.

During this time, I noticed that many of us are far removed from the earth, from a basic connection to ourselves, and from our own true nature. I noticed that when I had worked at that frenetic pace, I had always made time to go off on various adventures. This was the way I kept refilling my own tank and mitigating the effects of that fast-paced work life. I wanted to find a way to stay fully connected, and I didn't want to just keep putting a bandage on issues I stored within myself. I was attempting to shift the way I practiced medicine, because it was quite clear to me that every facility in Western medicine expects everyone to move at record speeds. I learned that healing becomes even more difficult if we don't take the time to be in contact with our bodies, our spirits, and the earth.

The earth has an energy—a vibration with amazing healing properties. Negatively-charged ions are created in abundance around plant life, bodies of water, and in nature. We take these negative ions in just by breathing while we are out in nature. They enter our blood streams and create a biochemical reaction that increases mood elevators in the brain. So, while walking upon the earth with its large water content beneath her, we bring a flow of healthy negative ions into ourselves. And if we have a buildup of unhealthy positive ions and any accompanying toxins, they flow out as we walk. This is how we naturally and organically take care of our systems while out walking in nature.

Negative ions have been found to assist with SAD (Seasonal Affective Disorder), as well as with depression. Scientists believe this happens because the negative ions that affect our mood are related to the chemical serotonin. The increased levels of serotonin in the brain provide a boost in our energy and help to relieve stress. Today, scientists have been referencing the wonderful benefits of nature's prescription when we get outside into the "green gym." Being out in nature is indeed one of the best forms of medicine for us all.

I KNEW that if I was to fully understand and take in the true art of medicine, along with what healing really meant and felt like, I needed to slow down enough to allow myself to fully heal, while living closer to and being more connected to the earth. The reality was I wasn't ready until then. I mean, how could I know what my body was feeling if I didn't stay still long enough to feel, connect, or take in what was happening within myself?

The fact that the ancient wisdom of TCM has been around far longer than the Western medicine approach has had a significant impact on me, and I knew that this ancient wisdom could easily be incorporated into my practice. The 5 Elements became a guide for me, a way to bring in all parts of the person, which is what is required so a person can fully heal. We are not a system unto ourselves—we are beings of wholeness connected on all levels in the universe, with our spirits at the helm. Attempts to separate our spirits from our bodies never seemed to work in my approach to healing.

The magic of healing begins when we connect to spirit and listen to our bodies, especially when it speaks to us. Sometimes it is only a faint whisper and we may choose to ignore it. However, if we negate these messages over time, or keep filling our busy minds with non-stop chatter, it will catch up with us. Today, I see more lost and disconnected souls than ever before. I see more disease in the body and more emotional unrest in young and old alike. We are all part of the universe, which makes us all interconnected. If we are living our lives alienated from our bodies and spirits, and if we are not connected to the earth, we will not get any healthier.

The body's innate wisdom provides us with an avenue to navigate, although we have to get in the game in order to participate. I wish that everyone may find a gentle way to stumble onto something that can provide them with new insight into their holdings, their pain, or their unrest, and that they can find a way back into connection with their body and spirit. It is my belief that the 5 Elements hold the key to our body's "safe"—that place within us where we store all of our unexpressed emotions and our life's traumas. All we have to do is make the choice to turn the key and open the door.

3

Do we have a choice about what gets passed down to us?

I AM FIRST GENERATION Irish with a strong family lineage drenched in the magic and mystery of the Emerald Isle. My mother's mother had a gift—she was a seer. When people died, she would see their light and would let their loved ones know when the person had crossed over. My grandmother had lots of these deeper knowings, and let's just say that anyone who had the pleasure of making her acquaintance received a blessing. My acceptance of unusual experiences may have something to do with my family origin.

My mother was born in County Mayo, Ireland—a place some refer to as "Ireland's Wild West." County Mayo sweeps along the "Wild Atlantic Way," with a breathtaking landscape imbued with the Emerald Isle's mystical essence. My mother came to the U.S. in 1952 at eighteen years of age, as did many others during that time period. In terms of family history, we didn't have much information about my dad's side of the family because my dad was primarily raised by his grandmother without a father. Thus, his lineage remains somewhat of a mystery.

I got a bit of clarity about my family history after exploring my heritage through an ancestry service. I discovered I'm 99.9% European.

The Celtic origin was quite high at eighty-six percent, with the remaining percentage points divided between Scandinavian, Italian, German, French, and Iberian. While much of this came down from my mother's side, it appears my dad likely had some Emerald blood in him as well. Interestingly, the highest percentage points of the other ethnicities I discovered were Neanderthal. The Neanderthal lineage seems to make sense, given my love and connection to the earth.

We all carry with us a link to our familial history, and each generation adds a new "branch" to the family tree, each providing a gift in our lives and in our hearts. The older we get, the more we appreciate how fleeting life is and how precious a gift our loved ones are. For me, prior to my dad's passing was an emotionally tender time. I had taken a month off for family medical leave to assist my mom and dad. My dad had been diagnosed with cancer a year prior and did well after he had completed treatment. The cancer had now returned, and it had metastasized. Dad decided to remain home; no more radiation or chemo—he'd had enough. I was the caretaker of our clan, and since I had learned quite a bit about my own inner workings (having done a lot of soul-work), I was comfortable being with my dad through this time. My mom was getting older and lifting and transferring my dad was not something I wanted for her, nor did she. My month-long leave was coming to an end, and Dad was getting thinner and weaker as his time here on earth became limited. Our last month together allowed us all to see and be with him in his truest spirit form, as my dad had found peace with his time ending here on earth. It was painfully beautiful.

With less than a week remaining of my leave, I said to my dad, "I must go back to work on Tuesday. But should you choose to leave by then, I will get another two weeks off for bereavement leave." He looked at me and said, "I will leave Tuesday." We never spoke of it again and left it at that.

Tuesday morning came. It was early, Mom was on the phone with a dear friend. She entered the room and shared, "Rosie just told me a joke." "Well, let's hear it!" I said. I sat on one side of Dad's bed holding his hand, and Mom sat on the other side, holding his other hand. She shared the joke and we laughed so hard...everything was all about the joy in that moment. While we were immersed in that fit of laughter, my dad chose to take his final breath.

We were filled with such joy, as well as tremendous sadness and loss—all compressed into that one brief moment. Just like life, I guess...it's filled with so many precious moments of joy and sorrow. When we choose to fully take life in—I mean life in its *entirety*—we never know where these experiences will take us.

Interestingly, my dad knew of his departure date, just as my maternal grandmother back in Ireland knew of hers. As I mentioned, she knew of many others' days of departure, too. I started to think about that. When we connect, I mean fully connect to our purest form as spirit, is it not plausible that we have direct access to our soul's comings and goings? My maternal grandmother was very connected to the land and to spirit—she was never without her rosary beads. I remember her with a smile, a song, and a sweet sparkle that shimmered throughout her entire being.

I WAS A YOUNG GIRL of seven on my first voyage to my mom's homeland. This was when I first met my Grandma. How she moved about on the land mesmerized me. She appeared to be filled with such joy in her effortless ways of being on and with the earth. A child enchanted by it all, I would follow her around while she did her chores. I never understood until I was much older, how much Grandma really walked! She walked to the well to fill buckets of water, which I recall was not that close to the house. She herded the cattle, gathered the hay, cut the turf for the fire, fed the chickens, collected the eggs, milked the cows, and on and on it went, day after day.

This mutual exchange between my grandmother and the land she lived on flowed effortlessly. By witnessing how my grandmother lived her life and took care of her home and land, I was shown her love and appreciation of all the gifts our dear Gaia provided her. My grandmother showed me how to move as one with the resonance of the earth's energies. My understanding of her provided me with a deeper understanding of myself. She was a woman of grace, who walked with spirit, enlivened with each step as she made her way through life.

Retracing the roots of my Irish heritage helped me to understand the deep longing and tremendous sense of connection I have with the earth, spirit, and the natural world. I was curious as to why I always had such a strong pull to Ireland. Had the fact that my mother had been transplanted here on American soil brought some instability to my root system? Had that contributed to me not being fully grounded here? I had come across some research once that discussed the idea that our ancestors have a direct correlation to our physical and emotional health that can be traced back through our lineage.

Later, when I learned about the intergenerational effects of trauma, I wondered—is there a correlation between what our ancestors endured and how we navigate in the world? Is there a larger picture? It may well be that we each come into this life fairly weighed down with ancestral baggage, even before we make our way into the world. One example is the case studies with Holocaust survivors. The researchers found that the stress hormone profiles of descendants of Holocaust survivors were different than "*normal;*" they had a predisposition to anxiety disorders. That research made me aware that many of us enter this life carrying the trauma (some known or unknown) of our ancestral lineage. These traumas may contain a hidden piece of our excess emotional baggage that has been stored within our physical, emotional, mental, or spiritual bodies.

The good news is that the beautiful aspects of our family lineages are part of us as well—we are all of it, the light and the dark. For example, innately, we may have a love of certain foods, traditions, genres of music, ceremonies, dances, rituals, or we may even have certain esoteric abilities. When we truly connect into these deeper parts of ourselves, it can enliven our spirits to feel expansive and joyous.

On the other hand, if we have been consciously or unconsciously cut off from these deeper parts of ourselves, that might explain why we can feel a bit off balance at times while moving through life. After tirelessly seeking for that something or someone outside myself, I realized I still felt this internal struggle and separation from source. I longed to nourish this part of myself, to find peace with myself, inside and out.

So, even though some of our choices are made for us when we come in, I believe our soul's longing continues to guide us forward... by guiding us back home to the fully embodied, expansive self that includes our entire mind, body, and spirit. Our spirit longs to be enlivened so we can make our way through life with effortless joy, peace, and balance.

I have spent the larger part of my life trying to understand what it means to fully accept myself and my way of being in the world. I recognize that I'm a unique person: spirited, somewhat quirky, and a bit magical. That's probably a good summation of me. I have often felt like I didn't fit quite right, as if my clothes were a bit too snug, making it hard for me to take in a full, deep breath. I wanted to go back to my ancestral roots to see what I could find—perhaps I would stumble upon some secret, lost along the way, that would help me to fit better in the world, to feel more comfortable in my own skin, to understand my gifts and the way in which I worked with people. It felt like I needed to go back and pull some weeds so I could get to the root of my own existence. I guess all of this searching was so that I could fully accept and love myself, just as I am.

When I discovered that my truest connection to source was by way of the natural world, an enormous weight was lifted from me. It was as if I had been given a hall pass with full access to "go out and play" in the world. I knew that when I walked gently upon the earth, I was completely cared for and at home in my body. When I was in right relation with Gaia—I was in right relation with myself. Mother

Nature had been calling to me for quite some time, but until then I hadn't been paying close enough attention.

If I go back in time and recall the various places I was living and working when Mother Nature spoke so strongly to me, it's uncanny. Perhaps these were all Mother Nature's way of getting my attention on my not so "straightforward" path, perhaps each time she "woke me up," she was guiding me to a missing piece of my elemental toolbox— guiding me ever closer to having all the tools I needed to assist people.

The first example I remember was a big snowstorm when I was a child, back East. It was the blizzard of 1978. It took weeks for areas to recover. I recall struggling through the snow, dragging my sled behind me to go to the market for some milk and bread for my family. I made it home in one piece, having learned for the first time in my young life the power of the elements. As a young nurse, I was living in Charlotte, North Carolina, and during Hurricane Hugo the first responders came to our home and used a chainsaw to cut their way through the fallen debris so I could get to work at the hospital. The gale force winds that devastated the area left a memorable imprint on me.

Another time, I was living in Southern California during the Northridge earthquake. I was thrown onto the bedroom floor when she struck. I saw firsthand what occurs during an earthquake... many people were left physically and emotionally traumatized. Then, just before Hurricane Katrina hit, I was asked to join IMSURT (International Medical Surgical Rescue Team), which I did. I ended up in New Orleans working as a provider in a MASH (Mobile Army Surgical Hospital) tent for two weeks. The enormous destruction from Katrina also shone a light on impoverished areas which were unknown until disaster hit. Throughout these catastrophic events, I was able to remain calm and bring healing to people in ways I could have never imagined.

Sadly, I have also been in two large fires that I will speak about later. I have also experienced a couple of small floods, one in my parents' home while I was visiting, and another in a condo I owned in Boston.

As you can see, all of the 5 Elements have been cast in many roles for me throughout the play of my life. I am so grateful I made it safely through each natural disturbance and was able to continue working and caring for people through each of them.

MY BOND with Mother Nature is strong. But I never understood her strange sense of humor or the ways in which she came knocking at my door until I finally opened that door and accepted her invitation to bring my whole self forward. For example, remember all those slit lamp exams I did? I thought that all those opportunities to use the slit lamp came to me so I could help improve other people's vision. But now I believe that it was my own vision that needed to be brought into better focus, to see life through a broader lens that accepts all aspects of self, other, and the universe at large.

Perhaps my internal struggle was (in part at least), my process of discovery, my way of becoming more finely tuned to what and who I am as an instrument of healing. Once I realized my personal style of healing is informed by the natural world, I finally came into my own. My coming into alignment with myself probably only made sense to me when I discovered that it was not what lay outside of me, or across the Atlantic, or even in the exam room that mattered. It was right beneath me all along—my connection to the deep wisdom and medicine of the earth and her many gifts. This is the journey that led me to the deeper aspects of myself, those places I never understood until now.

Just as the earth awaited my arrival, she awaits yours. Will you accept her invitation to step into the truth of who you really are?

4

My Journey into the Elements

"Nature itself is the best physician." —Hippocrates

WHERE DO YOU feel most at peace? Many people say it is when they are out in nature—experiencing the smells and sounds of the ocean, or perhaps resting against a beautiful oak or a majestic redwood. Nature has a way of calming us and bringing us back to a place of ease and comfort, and in her vastness, she makes our problems seem less significant. Nature always seems to find her way back into a state of balance, no matter what comes her way. She provides a cycle of nurturance, just as a mother does when she nurtures her child. As a result, we...or nature...flourish and blossom. In essence, our cycles are similar—one nurtures, one needs support. There is a reciprocity between us and the natural world that keeps us both in balance.

The opening of a beautiful nurturing cycle within the 5 Elements is depicted in the following sequence. As Fire burns, it creates the Earth. Then from the Earth we mine Metal. If Metal is heated and cooled, it creates condensation, which forms Water. As Water floods our Earth, it nourishes the land and creates bountiful forests, filled with Wood. Wood grows wild and free, and we can create Fire by rubbing two pieces of Wood together. Then the Fire warms our homes and nourishes our hearts.

The elements all intersect with one another and work together in some way, as seen in this generating cycle, providing support to one another (see chart at end of this chapter). The other cycle is that of controlling or opposing energies, with both cycles necessary as they interweave to create and balance everything in the universe. Just as the elements all interact in nature, they are woven through our lives and can show up as areas of excess and/or deficiency. So, in order to restore balance, we must work at finding ways to open and balance our systems in order to create more peace and harmony, inside and out.

When we allow our bodies to tune naturally into nature's rhythm, we tend to seek out what nourishes us and feeds us organically during certain seasons throughout the year. For example, picking something light and fresh to eat during the summer months, when we are more active, allows us to move easier. We tend to choose dense, rooted foods to assist us as we turn inward for rest and self-reflection through the darker days of winter. Harmonizing the body's natural ebb and flow with nature's rhythms creates a healthier, more finely-tuned body.

So, in order to understand ourselves as whole beings, we must understand the role that opposites play in creation. We are both the light and the dark, both male and female—also known as the Yin (female)/ Yang (male) aspects. There is never a day without a corresponding night. The Yin/Yang symbol represents opposites coming together in union with our duality, making it easier to see the symbiotic relationship we as human beings have with the elements. These contrasting aspects are all interconnected to make up our entire system (including the physical, mental, emotional, spiritual, and energetic levels).

To create balance within us, the elements work together collectively for the greater good of the whole, just as they do in the natural world. Each element also has its own way of opening or accessing its medicine. Every element has a season, a color, a sound, a climate, a direction, a flavor, a body part, and an emotion associated with it.

The 5 Elements made perfect sense to me—as a tool to help bring more clarity and wisdom to the deeper aspects of ourselves. The more

I worked with the elements, the more I saw how the natural world provides a mirror for us. It reflects what's going on in the body as well as in the world around us. The more I discovered these amazing (and relatively simple) ways of working with the elements, the more eager I was to bring them into my practice.

The following passage was taken from a piece written by Richard Rohr, about St. Bonaventure of Bagnoregio (1217-1274), a Franciscan philosopher and mystic. As I read this, I thought, *this is a wonderful summation of the Elemental cycles, and the struggles we endure in human form, finding our way to spirit.* Rohr says:

> Christ reveals the necessary cycle of loss and renewal that keeps all things moving toward ever further life. The death and birth of every star and atom is this same pattern of loss and renewal, yet this pattern is invariably hidden, denied, or avoided, and therefore must be revealed by Jesus—through his passion, death, and resurrection.

—Richard Rohr, "Christ is the Template for Creation"

These words provide us with an understanding that each of us is born as a star—seeking to bring forth more of ourselves in this life. We may fall ill, or somehow lose our way, which prevents us from bringing forth our full life cycles and manifesting our undeniable brilliance. The opportunities we have to uncover and reveal ourselves by way of these natural cycles of birth, death, and renewal keep us moving forward. If we dare to open our hearts and take part in this intricate web of connection, we experience a never-ending process of birthing ourselves anew, over and over. Our lives are not just about any one moment in time. Our lives are a series of encounters that bring us to deeper understandings of our truth, the truth that we are all interconnected and that each of us influences the unfolding of others' lives. It's just like in the natural world—everything is birthing and dying continually, through various seasons and cycles.

We are like roses that don't bloom in the same way every season. We must choose to spend time pruning our inner gardens, to let go of what has lived out its natural cycle, so that we can bring forward new blossoms…different blossoms. We all take part in learning about ourselves, all in our own unique fashion, all at our own time and pace. So, when bringing the elements in as a tool to provide new insights into what's going on in our world and in our body, one person may have a learning experience, while another person finds that the same experience opens them to release. Wherever we find ourselves in the moment is perfect. Just like the seasons, we are always shifting and changing.

I HAVE WITNESSED so much suffering in people, and I'm always looking to find ways to make people's journeys a little gentler. In my Western training, I saw each person as unique, and I realized that not everyone benefits from taking the "purple pill." As I added this little "cookbook" of the 5 Elements to my toolbox, and shared this knowledge with people, I noticed that they began to shift. They began to see and understand what their challenges were offering to teach them. Understanding the principles of the 5 Elements provided people with a different approach and meaning to their health challenges. They began to see the interactions between what was going on in their lives and how their body was speaking to them. They were discovering, in fact, that we are all part of nature, just as nature is part of us. And knowing this, they realized that they could work to create a more balanced existence, even through the most turbulent times.

I remember having someone who wanted to participate in a journey (workshop) I offered. He asked, "Can you provide me with a tip about what it is you do?" I said, "When you go out today and make your way on the land, ask to be directed to an area on the earth. An area or place you can gather something about yourself that will provide an essential piece for you here and now on your journey."

I saw him the next day and he said, "It was the wildest thing! When I left you, I ended up going over to an overburdened peach tree. After almost an hour of pruning back the tree, it hit me. My life right now, and the way I am living it, is overburdened. I have a bad back, work far away from home, have relationship issues, manage various properties for someone and share custody with my ex, which is a bit trying." I chuckled and said, "Mother Nature never seems to disappoint." It is up to us whether or not we make the conscious effort to take the next steps toward change. If we can trust enough to loosen the reins and allow spirit to make its way in, things usually turn out far better than we could ever imagine.

After I completed a journey with a group of people, this passage came through me: "Our truest nature to fully connect, heal, and grow is to be mirrored by something that reflects our full essence. I believe the natural world is that ideal mirror." I realized that when we can sit still and *be* with Mother Nature, who is always in the present moment, she reflects who we really are without judgment. If we can trust in her guidance and support, we may be surprised by the deep wisdom and medicine she holds. When it comes to our health, if we look to nature, she can lead us forward and show us a different way to heal. In some more serious situations, we might even need to find a new way to keep us in the game of life. Nature can guide us back to our own body's healing power and wisdom.

In my work as a healer, throughout my career I have answered to a variety of names—"energy healer," "nurse," "spiritual guide," "medicine-woman," "nurse practitioner," and sometimes "doctor" (when a person has no understanding of what a nurse practitioner is). No matter what people call me, I always know my work is not to fix or to save anyone. Instead, it is to provide information and understanding to help people restore their health and come back into alignment with their own true nature. I bring people an awareness of elemental nature not only to help them find new avenues to health, but also to help them digest the medicine the 5 Elements offer.

There are many natural modalities for healing that use the 5 Elements as a basis for their healing system. For example, for thousands of years, the Chinese have been using Acupuncture as a first line treatment for a variety of illnesses. I do not utilize Acupuncture in my work, although I did discover the benefits of Acupressure when the French healer I went to squeezed my toes to release my sinus points!

Acupressure is a useful tool to augment your healing system (though it is not necessary when working with the elements), and to assist when certain symptoms are present. To get a sense of how this modality works, you can begin to locate tender points on your body and then breathe and massage into those areas. Many of these points can be found on your ears, hands, and feet, and they correlate to the energy pathways of the meridians* in the body. I use this in my practice when someone has an acute sinus issue or a lingering cough, and sometimes I use it for patients who have headaches. Occasionally, I will use Acupressure when someone is having trouble dealing with certain emotions.

I have also found EFT (Emotional Freedom Technique) a useful tool with people who are having difficulty handling their emotions. EFT is a tapping technique where people tap along the end points of the body's meridians while speaking aloud their specific challenge. I found this useful with people experiencing anxiety, inconsolable tears, a limiting belief, and/or feeling frozen or stuck in certain areas physically or emotionally. It can calm a person's entire system relatively easily. It's not hard to learn, takes only a few minutes to do, and works wonders with opening up stuck energy.

The work of Master Mingtong Gu, who incorporates sound with Qigong, a practice of gentle forms of movement, also assists in opening blockages. (The teachings by Master Mingtong Gu are based on the work of Dr. Pang Ming.) Please check out the reference section

---

*Meridians are pathways that carry energy through the body, similar to how the arteries and veins carry the blood. When I looked up "meridian" in the dictionary, I found it fascinating. Its…"primary meaning is a giant imaginary circle on the surface of the earth." Our dear universe, she is so humorous in the numerous ways she supports us as we make our way through life.

for more information on this tool. Qigong, EFT, Acupressure, Acupuncture—all of these methods and practices are useful and work well with the ancient medicine of the 5 Elements. See what works best for you!

I K N O W I don't come close to giving the elements or this ancient tradition their just due. For me, blending Western medicine and the ancient medicine of TCM's 5 Elements (along with other energy healing modalities) is my way of seeing how the "art" of medicine truly works. The 5 Elements have proven to be so beneficial in people's healing that it is now a vital part of my practice. Today, Western medicine continues as it has for many years, except the time allotted to see each person has been reduced. This time restriction makes it difficult for me to see and bring forth the entire person. And, as I've discovered, I'm not keen on not having enough time to drop down into the place whence all healing is derived—the heart. It's in the heart that the exchange of healing occurs and the well of compassion resides.

Whatever 5 Element energy healing technique you may favor for your healing journey or practice, remember that they are all used to help open our systems—to avoid blocking and containing our life force, which takes up far more time and energy in the long run. So many of us are seeking ways to make it through life's ups and downs (though we know that life wouldn't be life without them both). If we can learn to ride life's waves while staying present with its constant ebb and flow, we will continue to grow and create more balance in our lives.

As you make your way through this book, it's important to understand that all 5 Elements work in unison. In order to understand the whole system, you need first to understand each element separately. Because it will be easiest for you to take in each of the element's unique qualities and benefits separately, the information is presented one element at a time throughout the remaining chapters.

There are many paradigms used to teach the 5 Elements. I am bringing forward the way I use them, which guides my work as a practitioner, whether I am in an office or out on the land. I invite you to join me in applying the miraculous healing power of the 5 Elements to your own healing journey or practice. Welcome to the world of energy healing and the 5 Elements!

5 ELEMENTS

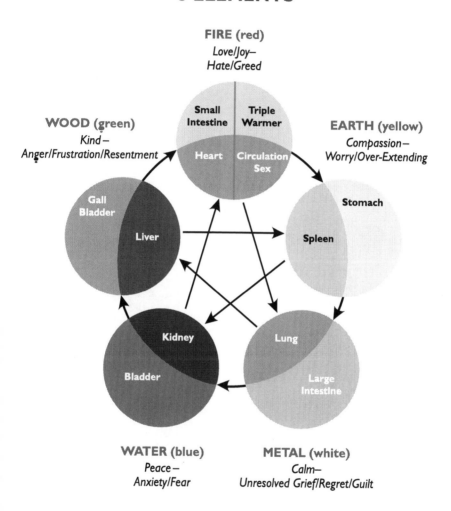

FIRE (red)
Love/Joy–
Hate/Greed

WOOD (green)
Kind –
Anger/Frustration/Resentment

EARTH (yellow)
Compassion–
Worry/Over-Extending

Small Intestine

Triple Warmer

Heart

Circulation Sex

Gall Bladder

Stomach

Liver

Spleen

Kidney

Lung

Bladder

Large Intestine

WATER (blue)
Peace –
Anxiety/Fear

METAL (white)
Calm–
Unresolved Grief/Regret/Guilt

5

The Earth,
an unending well of compassion

THE EARTH is the place where we begin, and in time, we return to the source from which we came. Earth is the element we walk upon daily, if we are fortunate to be able to do so. The emotional components of this element have to do with *sympathy* and *empathy*. The earth is the element of relationships—we give without needing to receive, and we receive without needing to give. When we come into harmony with the earth, we build harmony within ourselves, as well as with our family and community.

The earth element is located along our stomach and spleen meridians. We break down and digest our food in our stomachs. When all is good with the stomach and digestion, a person feels satiated without needing to overfeed themselves or others. The spleen is where we filter our blood and it is part of our immune system, helping us ward off certain infections. The earth element opens with *singing*. When in right relationship with the self and all beings, music naturally flows through you.

The Color of the Earth Element is
YELLOW.

When the earth element is in balance, we are vibrant, nurturing, and compassionate. People with balanced earth elements are known for their calm temperaments and their roles as peacemakers. They are generous and thoughtful and walk through life centered and grounded, connected to self and source.

If this element is off balance, our emotions may turn to worry, obsession, or others may perceive us as being needy or as meddling into others' lives. An off-balance earth element can bring up feelings of insecurity and issues of worthiness. Depression can be seen with this imbalance; it is related to the inability to take in the beauty of life or not finding meaning or purpose in life.

Boundary issues can also be seen with an imbalanced earth element. Have you ever felt your life force being sucked from you when you are around a certain person or persons? You may be drawn to these people's energy fields, in order to learn things about yourself and your own boundaries. Remember Mr. Einstein's theory, like-attracts-like? In these and similar situations, I think the universe has a field day with us, continually demonstrating just where we may be out of balance, and having others come forward to teach us about the imbalances within us.

Having an out of balance earth element can manifest in many ways. For example, you may have issues with certain people or with members of your family, which get you feeling sick to your stomach or tied up in knots. Or, maybe you overextend yourself to the point that there is nothing left for *you*. The true meaning of taking care of one's self (self-care), may be hard for you to comprehend. Muscle complaints and soft tissue issues along with anemia, blood cancers, or certain infections may all relate to an imbalance in the earth element.

Similarly, you may have food sensitivities, digestion problems such as heartburn, bloating, appetite issues, or an eating disorder. The pancreas is associated with this element—it assists with digestion and the regulation of blood sugar, such as in the case of diabetes. Is there enough sweetness in your life? Now, this isn't to say that everyone with diabetes or digestion issues has problems in relationships, or that you may not understand how to take care of yourself, but these things could play a part. I propose that if you have reacted to anything I have said on this topic so far, there might be issues around the topic you have reacted to...and that may be a clue indicating it's an area for you to work on. Again, that funny universe will show us parts of ourselves— whether we are paying attention or not!

An earth imbalance may also occur if we had an unclear understanding of what it was to feel supported and nurtured by a parent or guardian in our early lives. This may contribute to not understanding what being satiated truly feels like in life and in one's body. It could also play a role with our inability to accept the ground beneath us as a place we feel safe and secure. If this is how an earth imbalance manifests, oral addictions like overeating or smoking can be used as a means to self-nurture. But in these futile attempts to self-nurture, we end up not understanding how to receive or take in nourishment for ourselves, because we never understood what an effortless exchange of love and nurturance meant or felt like on a cellular level. So, searching for what it means to be truly fulfilled becomes a part of our journey.

When newborn babies are touched, they will naturally turn towards the source of the stimulus and make a sucking motion. This so-called "rooting reflex" is an indicator as to whether or not the child will be successful with breastfeeding. I often wonder if a weak rooting reflex might also be an indicator that a child will exhibit an earth imbalance later in life. Observing such traits in babies could serve as an "early warning system," allowing parents to take action to assist the child in learning early grounding techniques as they make their way into the world— whole and confident.

Interestingly, the powerful hormone oxytocin gets stimulated during breastfeeding. Oxytocin is considered "the love hormone," and it plays a significant role in maternal bonding and building trust between mother and child. Bringing this awareness to mothers who are not able to breastfeed, or who had a child with difficulty rooting onto the breast, would be invaluable. We could incorporate grounding activities with children during their first years of life, assisting to bring them into their bodies and onto the earth more fully, which would benefit their health long term.

Over many years, I have noticed that it is difficult to overcome an earth imbalance—especially for women. This element is related to our muscles and soft tissue, which includes our breast tissue. The breasts were designed to feed and nurture our children, as well as for pleasure. According to Dr. Christiane Northrup, women who tend to be most at risk for breast cancer are those who have difficulty nurturing themselves and receiving pleasure. I have spent the last couple of years providing energy medicine once a week for our local cancer center. I noticed the majority of breast cancers were on the left breast, which constitutes the highest percentage of breast cancer overall. It is interesting that our left side energetically is the side where we receive and take in—the feminine receptive side of the body. The right side is the masculine side—we give from and let go from the right sides of our bodies. I have found that for many women, the ability to *receive* is one of the most challenging lessons of all. As Dr. Northrup says:

> *The first thing you need to understand is you have to learn how to receive—how to receive rest, how to receive pleasure—and that's going to be the primary intervention that I would do. This is the biggest stumbling block for women: we're so afraid of appearing selfish. We import it through alcohol and sugar when we can import it directly through self- love, meditation, exercise, and good sex, which you can do with yourself.*

I took some women from the cancer center on a journey to a beautiful spot in Jack London Park in Glen Ellen, California.

One courageous women in her late forties who joined us that day had come into the world with a difficult start. She was adopted and uprooted a few times before landing in a permanent home. Her birth mother had died, as did another mother she ended up with right after her natural mother passed. Then, her third mother passed away while she was in her teens. Her place of support and nurturance had been taken away so many times when she was starting out in the world. It was hard to imagine this happening to anyone. With a history like this, how would one begin to trust and allow one's self to feel safe enough to receive in the world?

This lovely woman was dealing with breast cancer on her left breast at the time of our journey. I listened to the early accounts of her life, and it was obvious to me she had an earth imbalance. She had been discovering how to bring herself to receive in areas that were foreign to her because her own needs were left out of many equations during her childhood. It was remarkable to witness her strength and determination to heal, and I was honored to be able to work with her during her year of treatment.

On the day of our journey, we made our way into a circle. It was a beautiful day, calm and sunny, in a spot supported and surrounded by an amazing grove of redwood trees. As she began to share, leaves started to drop from the trees. It was as if a rainstorm of leaves came falling down only on her, no one else. It was dramatic—leaves began showering her, as if she was shedding and letting go of what had already died in her. She was ready for composting, allowing her next season of change to come forth. Surrounded by women, the strength of the redwoods, and supported by the earth beneath her, this was a place her system could truly receive and allow this nurturance.

When we allow ourselves the opportunity to truly let go, it can leave us feeling exposed and vulnerable. But this is the time when healing can take place and something new and different can begin to emerge from the dross of our former selves. As mythologist, Joseph Campbell, shares so eloquently in, *Sukhavati, A Mythic Journey*:

So, yield to what is coming. We're in a freefall into the future. We don't know where we're going. Things are changing so fast, and always when you're going through a long tunnel… But all you have to do to transform your hell into a paradise is to turn your fall into a voluntary act. It's a very interesting shift of perspective…joyfully participate in the sorrows and everything changes.

So, in our healing journeys, we can open ourselves up to the cycles of the seasons. After a life of hanging on, squeezing our life force from life itself, we can begin to take part in this new shift of energy, and allow change to come. As autumn lightens its load, we can rest upon the earth's bed of leaves, allowing her to support and nurture us. In the winter, we can rest and recuperate, and in the springtime, we can emerge from our old selves and begin anew to take part in our shifting energy, as we blossom into summer and the fullness of who we truly are.

Recently, I have been receiving music recordings from the woman who had the rainstorm of leaves fall upon her on the day of our journey. Singing keeps the earth element open to allow these new energies to flow. But whichever element you are balancing, just know that once you start to work with these transformative energies, opportunities for growth will come from the hell that once bound you. What no longer serves you begins to fall away, bringing in a life of new prospects and new opportunities to embrace the paradise that surrounds you.

Many of us began our lives in homes that only spoke and understood the language of lack. The vocabulary of wholeness was not in our teachings because it was not in our parents' "handbook" when they came in. We cannot go back in time, but we can begin again and relearn a new language—a language of love. Learning to speak the language of love allows us to give and receive from a nourished place within ourselves as we begin to understand what it feels like to be nurtured and to nurture from a place of wholeness, inside and out.

Enrolling ourselves in this school of love begins with realizing that we are sacred vessels made of compassion, love, and respect. This enables us to create strong foundations, grounded in spiritual strength. We enliven and brighten our entire system when we fill ourselves with loving, compassionate, respectful energy. Remember Albert Einstein and the laws of physics? Einstein explained that we can match the frequency of the reality we want. If we can begin to create love for ourselves, our hearts will beat true and attract others whose hearts beat in harmony with ours. This like-attracts-like energy will ripple out to our family, friends, our relationships—and then out into the world. It's a win-win-win situation.

I WOULD LIKE to share a story of a beautiful, fifty-eight-year-old woman I'll call Chrissy, who recently passed away from pancreatic cancer. The magnitude of this story is difficult to absorb, although the imbalance of the earth element displayed in her story was profound.

I remember first meeting Chrissy in a class she held on learning the basics of working with clay. As she spoke, she sat in a chair, her feet dangling—she never quite touched down upon the earth. As a worker of clay, the earth was indeed her friend, but she kept her distance, never quite allowing herself to connect fully. She spoke to the class, while partly in separation from herself and the earth. In observing her partner— I'll call him Dan—it was evident to me that he was very much her mirror. Chrissy did not have an issue with alcohol, nor did she have the genetic link that could attribute to pancreatic issues.

After Chrissy passed, I had the opportunity to visit her home. I found it to be quite disorganized. Seeing the place where she dwelled in such disarray led me to think about her illness in relation to the 5 Elements perspective. The home within ourselves, when it is not built from a grounded source, can spill over into other areas of our life—into the physical home in which we live, into our relationships and family, and into our place of work. If we start out in life with a solid connection to the earth beneath us, however, we can handle more of life's ups and downs.

Many times, we look esthetically pleasing on the outside, with our clothes and make up "just so." Our homes appear neat and tidy to all our neighbors. But sometimes, we end up "playing house" and miss out on what our internal furnishings can feel like when we are living in a truly supported, nourishing, and connected structure. When living from an ungrounded place—especially when we are detached from source, both inside and out— it becomes difficult to stay healthy. But if we choose to take part in harvesting life from both the heavens and the earth—to be one with nature once again, we can take root, grow in balance, and create better overall health. As author Deepak Chopra says in *Journey into Healing*, "To be one with Nature again is vital—it allows inner and outer nature to blend, healing a separation that never existed in the first place."

I believe it is time for these understandings to come forward to assist us in ensuring that our children begin their lives fully embodied and grounded. For example, Chrissy may have been a beautiful little girl, dancing and twirling around in her youth—all the while unable to fully plant down on the earth. If Chrissy had understood that she was living in an ungrounded state and had noticed the first signs of her imbalance, she could have addressed them and possibly aided in preventing this devastating illness.

If only we had an awareness of how starting out disconnected and not fully embodied can impact our health. Holding this awareness may assist us in preventing many other ailments that may occur due to an imbalanced earth element.

As you make your way in the world, I would ask you to bring in some basic grounding activities into your daily life—especially when going through times of struggle. My hope is that as you begin to use some simple grounding methods for yourself (please refer to the Recommendation section), you would then share them with others, especially when you notice an earth imbalance. Imagine bringing these exercises into our kindergartens, classrooms, and pediatrician's offices. There are so many places they could be incorporated! So many of us oversee the lives of many—we are all guardians of one another on this journey. We never know the impact this could have down the road, if we made these teachings part of our educational programs and health care paradigms.

I encourage you to start with yourself—get firmly planted, grounded, and centered on the earth. When you are grounded, you automatically provide a mirror for the children in your world to see themselves reflected as solid, whole, rooted individuals—making their way as confident beings in the world. Wow, what a world this could be!

WHEN I WAS VISITING my mother recently, she shared with me a childhood memory of a time a teacher asked her to participate in a poetry reading. She told her grandmother, who owned the local shop, about the invitation. She was going to pass on the reading because she had no shoes or proper clothes to wear. Her grandmother promised she would purchase a dress and a pair of shoes for my mother. But her grandmother didn't follow through, so my mother didn't attend the reading. When the teacher asked my mother why she didn't show up, my mother was standing in the store with her grandmother. My mother said without hesitation, "I could not go in rags and without any shoes on my feet."

Having learned for the first time that my mother grew up without any shoes, I cried myself to sleep for three nights. On the third day, I said to my mother, "I'm feeling so sad that you had no shoes growing up." She looked at me and said, "But why? No one had any shoes back then. We were no different than anyone else."

I asked her about the poem she would have read, and it came to her like it was yesterday. "*O, Ireland! Isn't it grand you look...Like a bride in her rich adornin'....*" The poem is called "Dawn on the Irish Coast," also known as "The Exiles Return," by Irish writer John Locke. I ended up printing the poem, so we could have our own poetry reading that day. As she read it aloud, the tears flowed from us both.

I could feel the depths of where that poem touched her, as it did me. When my mother finished reading the poem, I commented on what a beautiful outfit she was wearing, shoes and all. Our tears quickly turned to laughter.

My mother said, "I think my attire was perfect for my reading, and no one would have made fun of my clothes." I laughed and cried some more. The pain that surfaced as she read allowed me the opportunity to open to the pain of her holdings, and to the pain of my own. The truth was that her beginnings were my beginnings. The ancestral wounds of our pasts come through us in a variety of forms, though they don't have to stay locked away or hidden. I was fortunate to witness this healing for my mother and blessed with this opportunity to heal this piece for myself. Those holdings can continue to keep our hearts closed or contained, preventing us from healing and opening to our fullest expressions of love.

I had a hard time digesting that story and feeling the tremendous suffering my parents endured—and the suffering so many of our parents and ancestors bore. Their hierarchy of needs was different than ours—they sought only for the basic provisions in life. I now understand that as a child, that worldview was instilled in me. Back then, to be nourished meant to be able to meet the necessities of the *external self*. Today, we in the western world have a different perspective. We have discovered the true meaning of being deeply nourished. We can feed our internal cravings as well, by tapping into a spirit-filled well, a spring of nurturance filled with love and compassion. I feel blessed knowing that my internal structure needs a solid foundation supported by both spirit and matter, nourished by the heavens and the earth. In part, this was the journey of my soul that I chose to discover this lifetime.

WHEN I CONSIDERED my mother's system (and the many other people during that time in history) and the strength of her constitution, I was struck by their relationship with the earth, and what that must have looked and felt like in their lives. The earth assisted them on the deepest levels, providing them much-needed nourishment and lands filled with tremendous healing frequencies. Back then, the earth's soil was alive and flourishing with abundant, healthy, negative ions. Living so close to the earth in a land rich with vital nutrients provided my mother with a strong constitution—and this strength and fortitude was handed down to me. I am grateful for that gift.

Today we see so much torture and damage brought into our earth's soil, and its lack of nutrients is apparent in many of us. Our world is wrought with disease and illness, along with staggering amounts of depression and anxiety. Are the anguish, pains, and emotional toxins we hold within us due in part to the fact that we no longer walk barefoot upon our Earth? We move at record speeds, with no time to take ourselves or the earth in. I believe that we avoid the earth's healing energies at the cost of our bodies, minds, and spirits.

The earth and all the other elements continually provide for us, without judgment and without discrimination. It does not matter what race, creed, color, gender, or religion we are—no one person is any different than anyone else. Shoes or not, all are welcome.

> *"In this earth*
> *In this soil*
> *In this pure field*
> *Let's not plant any seed*
> *Other than seeds*
> *Of Compassion and Love."*
> —Rumi

6

Metal, the true gem that resides in each of us

etal has the ability to be shaped and refined into the purest of forms. When we tend to the precious metal within us, it comes forward as inner strength that shines bright for all to witness.

This element has to do with our spirituality. It is the place we choose to find our connection with all of life. The person with a balanced metal element is accepting, methodical, and calm.

The metal element is located along our lung and large intestine meridians. The lungs' main function is our respiratory health; our breath is what allows us to take in all of life. We breathe in the oxygen produced by our plants and as we exhale, we breathe out excess carbon dioxide, which in turn feeds our plant world.

The large intestine, also called the colon, is the place of elimination—a place to let go of what is no longer useful for us. This element also has to do with our body hair and our skin. The skin, which is the largest organ and acts as a layer of protection, is an external filter for our body. It allows us to import the sun's energy and nutrients. Both our physical skin as well as our spiritual skin need tending.

When our self as source shines bright, our spirit finds unity in our way of being with ourselves and others. Then we can breathe easier, and our elimination systems release waste products without strain. The metal element opens with crying or deep sighing.

The Color of the Metal Element is *WHITE*.

When your metal element is in balance, you are inspirational and open. You can allow the natural evolution of life's rhythm to flow through you. You can process grief, as you are able to let go fully and surrender to life's flow. You have good self-esteem and a deep, inner strength. When it comes to the universal order of life, you are ethical and moral.

When the metal element is not in balance, one may have an unexplained fear of death. You may be grief stricken, experience ongoing depression, or have some form of longstanding regret or feelings of guilt. Chronic feelings of guilt can be a byproduct of your upbringing—a generational torch that gets handed down to you from your ancestors.

If your metal is out of balance, you may have issues like asthma, airborne allergies, frequent colds, a cough, or chronic respiratory symptoms. You could experience an exacerbation of these symptoms around the anniversary of a loss—for example, you might get bronchitis yearly. If you are unable to let things go, you may end up being constipated (or the opposite, having diarrhea), or you might suffer with symptoms of an irritable bowel. With an imbalanced metal element, problems like eczema, skin rashes, or body hair issues can arise.

ONE DAY I walked into an exam room to meet a beautiful fourteen-year-old girl who had come for a physical examination. I'll call her Amber. She was accompanied by a female guardian, no parent in sight. I surmised that something was amiss in her family unit, so I chose not to start with the obvious (her home life).

Amber had a pale complexion overall, she made minimal eye contact, and she sat with a slightly hunched upper back. I began her intake.

"Do you have any medical issues or take any medications?" I asked. Amber shared she had asthma and used an inhaler when she was active or in gym class. She also used a cream once in a while when she had a rash on her skin. "When did you start using your inhaler?" I asked. Amber didn't skip a beat and shared that she had started using it at eight years old. "What happened when you were eight?" I asked. She responded that it was when her grandfather had died. "Were you close?" I asked. Without hesitation, Amber answered, "Yes."

"Who lived in your home while you were growing up?" I asked. Amber shared that she had lived with her grandfather (until he died), her mother, and her grandmother. "Did you and your grandfather do anything fun together? Perhaps there was a favorite song you liked to listen to or sing?"

Surprised that I would even ask her such a thing, Amber replied "Yes!" Without skipping a beat, she shared that she had a little plastic keyboard and had a song they sang together. I asked if she would share it with me, and she didn't waste a second. The song came pouring out, along with her tears. Her cheeks pinked right up, as if her heart was bursting open right in front of us. A weight had lifted—the burden of her grief lightened, and fresh, oxygenated blood came swishing through her system. Amber had learned how to hold and contain her emotions, although her body's reaction was causing her lungs to restrict and her skin to erupt.

My heart was heavy. Amber had been without her beloved grandfather and her father was not part of her life. Amber's guardian and I were deeply moved, and I still tear up today remembering this child. Amber's opening moved each of us—it was a gift. It was amazing to witness how beautifully she dropped down into her heart, and how that allowed her a chance to open and begin to grieve. As the song came forward, Amber's body-wisdom followed, moving her to tears, so she could release some of her stored energy.

The metal element opens with tears and singing opens the element of earth. One can see how the body intuitively knows how to come back into its natural state when the opportunity presents itself. In my many years of doing this, I have noticed that a person never goes to a place they can't handle. Ultimately, we choose to allow our systems to open.

I realized that the unprocessed grief Amber stored appeared to have manifested quickly within her physical body. Also, it was interesting that her breathing difficulties were exercise-induced— occurring during those times she moved her body and had fun. The sadness she was experiencing was not allowing the energy of joy to trickle in—her lungs stopped her. Amber's asthma had developed only a month after the loss of her grandfather. Was this a direct correlation, or just a coincidence?

I took more of Amber's history and learned that her grandmother was on oxygen at home for a chronic lung condition. *Does the length of time an illness has been in the family correlate to the speed at which the pathology develops?* I wondered. *Is this all due to the loss of her grandfather? Or does it stem from a long line of grief, regret, or guilt in her family lineage?* I also thought about the many people who are born with reactive airway disease or asthma, and the many other conditions we come in with when we are born. Sometimes our physical challenges can go unexplained; it can be hard to decipher the reasons we carry certain conditions. These are indications that can lead us to more places to heal within ourselves and our lineage.

That day, I handed Amber a prescription for an inhaler. "When and if you need your inhaler," I said, "I invite you to sing the song you shared with your grandfather. See if that helps your breathing." I also taught her about conscious breathwork. This is a great tool that can assist in calming the system and works quite well whether or not you have breathing issues.

As a practice, breathwork has a variety of benefits. There is no cost for air—and breathwork helps to soothe many different ailments. So many of us are not even aware of how off balance we become with our daily stressors. When you take the time to slow your breath down, even for a few minutes a day, it can help you reset. I encourage breathwork as part of any self-care starter kit. A simple breathing technique I share with people is a 4-4-4 exercise:

As always, we begin with our feet firmly planted on the ground. We begin taking a deep breath in for the count of four, breathing in from the core of the earth. Allow your system to receive the earth's nurturing energies, then hold your breath for a count of four. Next, exhale for a count of four. While doing this, ask your body to compost or let go of what you no longer wish to carry, and send it back to the earth.

When I share this exercise with others, I breathe right along with them, breathing in through the nose and exhaling through the mouth. As I demonstrate this technique to show how easy it is, it provides me with an opportunity to slow myself down. It also helps to clear the mind. If the Navy SEALs use breathwork before any mission they go on, I think we can give ourselves a moment to do the same. As Dr. Andrew Weil says, "The single most effective relaxation technique I know is conscious regulation of breath."

In my office that day, as Amber's heart began pumping with a new strength, her vascular beds filled as renewed energy moved through her entire system, resulting in her new, rosy complexion. If we had not spoken about Amber's asthma in the exam room, and if we had not addressed the loss of her grandfather, Amber would not have had much of an opportunity to release her grief.

I haven't known many people who don't want to bring more life back to themselves and to find more balance in the process. If our spirit is not acknowledged or spoken to, then our spiritual muscles can't develop. That day, Amber and I spoke about where she could find a place that brought her peace—a place she felt at home within herself and her surroundings. Amber told me that she liked to sit by a tree and write. I encouraged her to do that.

When we allow ourselves to take time out for ourselves, we can begin a practice that allows our spirit room to breathe and to take life in. Perhaps it is the start of a daily meditation, allowing our bodies to slow down and reconnect with ourselves. As Deepak Chopra says, "To make the right choices in life, you have to get in touch with your soul. To do this, you need to experience solitude, which most people are afraid of, because in the silence you hear the truth and know the solutions."

When I asked Amber what she missed from home, she shared that she missed her dog. Her dog had brought her joy. After our visit, she made plans with her guardian to visit a farm across from her boarding home that was full of animals. I had already shared with Amber about how grounding into the earth could help nourish her system. For Amber, these recommendations—singing, doing breathwork, grounding, quiet contemplation, and spending time outside and with animals—were all ways to allow more of herself to come forward.

Many times, I provide people with a handout, an illustration of an element circle, and I recommend that they get quiet and consider which element may be out of balance at that time. When we begin to release and let go of our holdings, we create a space that needs to be filled. So, being outside in the natural world, or spending time with the beautiful animal kingdom, are ways to provide our systems with new *"filling stations"* of peace, love, and joy. And as we get still and calm our minds and our hearts, we can take the time to *"just breathe."*

TODAY, most of us live in a fairly oxygen-deprived state. And if our bodies are deprived of oxygen, we create illness and disease. Without our breath, there is no life. Our spirit is, in part, our breath of life. While the spiritual parts of ourselves are not spoken about as part of medicine—because spirituality is not looked at as a science—I still find it difficult to leave this part of a person outside of the exam room. We may have learned, for example, to speak about this aspect of our lives only when we visit our place of worship. Some of these places speak about regimented belief systems that are tightly bound with constraints. Other places of worship are filled with beautiful ceremonies and messages that bring us closer to source than any other time during our week.

After our weekly session at our church, temple, synagogue, or other spiritual gathering areas, we feel renewed, back in balance. This is why I believe many people live in an oxygen-deprived, spirit-deprived state. Our spirits are not meant to be acknowledged for only an hour on our weekly days of worship. Is the rest of our week meant to be spirit-free? I recommend a daily dose of spiritual awareness as part of our healing journey. I believe it to be a crucial, missing prescription in our practice of medicine. Embracing our body, mind, and spirit together, and living in relationship with all living matter allows our spirits to take form. It's a part of our existence (on all levels) that is necessary to tap into and nurture, so that the deepest parts of ourselves can truly heal.

Working with the metal element can bring up a lot for individuals. Some reasons for this can be obvious—for example, the loss of a loved one. As I mentioned previously, the metal element opens with tears. But society has a somewhat unspoken rule about crying—in a word, it's *unacceptable*. People apologize for crying, they hold back their tears, or they excuse themselves. If we don't feel safe enough to shed our tears, we won't feel safe enough to heal. The energy it takes to contain tears is far more restrictive than releasing them and allowing them to flow. Yet these societal taboos have endured for centuries, and they shape our lives, our bodies, and our health.

The weight of the holdings of our lineages affect us profoundly. For example, there are the regrets of not returning home, the shame in having no shoes, and the guilt that others place upon us when we decide to try something new. We are afraid to release the feelings we hold onto because of the consequences of expressing our deepest emotions. What if we lose as a result? But sometimes our grief, regrets, or guilt may be even more significant than the loss of something or someone. Until we allow ourselves the time to open and heal past holdings, we contribute to the generational stagnation of our entire familial energetic systems (our physical, emotional, and spiritual bodies). Releasing is the natural progression of things—yet our societal protocols stop us from allowing our natural rhythms, encouraging us not to release but instead to hold on.

Throughout the many cycles in nature, the earth never seems to hold on—it's just part of nature's evolution. When it's time to let go, nature just lets go. Death is part of nature's way of letting go. We can see a fear of death within a metal element imbalance. Death is hard for many to speak about, let alone process.

I remember sitting with a daughter and her mother who was not long for this world. The daughter, whom I'll call Debbie, spoke about her mother's nutritional needs and her limited mobility. Her mother, whom I'll call Ann, was lying supine on the bed, present but limited in her speech. I asked Debbie if she had anything she wanted to ask or share with her mother before she passed. Debbie started to tear up, then held back, not allowing her emotions to flow in front of her mother. I turned to Ann and asked her the same thing—did she want to share anything with her daughter, Debbie? No words were spoken. Then Debbie took hold of her mother's hand. So much was communicated between mother and daughter with that small gesture.

When we take the time to acknowledge one another from the heart, the place we so often want to avoid, it can heal places in us that words can never express. To stop and acknowledge one another allows us to begin the process of letting go, which ends up making more room for our love to be felt and more space for our hearts to heal.

Embracing the cycle of death/loss can allow and welcome a new season of growth and of change to come forward—so we can take in a full breath of life or allow a life lived to be set free. If we hold back or hold onto our grief, or hold onto people in our lives, or hold onto thoughts that no longer serve us, we can become a garbage can full of toxins that we store within the many parts of ourselves. These toxins will decay our spirits and make their way into our bodies. If we continue holding this death and decay, we invite in the process of illness and disease. It may be time to ask yourself, "What am I holding onto?"

> *"Don't run away from grief, o' soul.*
> *Look for the remedy inside the pain,*
> *because the rose came from the thorn*
> *and the ruby came from a stone."*
> —Rumi

7

Water, a place that reflects our truest self

W ATER FLOWS beneath the surface—into spaces we enter for deep introspection and from which we later emerge with a renewed curiosity about life. This element can bring us to the depths of our soul, to uncover our essence and ancestral wisdom. Water is the element of learning and teaching. From it, we gather knowledge to share with others and the world. The water element relates to our vital, life-force energy, our internal power.

The adult human body is made up of about sixty percent water, and the majority of the natural world is made up of water. This element is located along our kidney and bladder meridians. Our kidneys filter our blood, remove excess fluid, and help us flush out impurities. The kidney produces urine, which our pouch-shaped organ, the bladder, holds. This element opens up with the sound of groaning as it vibrates through the body.

The Color of the Water Element are
DEEP BLUE and BLACK.

When this element is in balance within you, you are introspective, have a quiet mind, and possess the temperament of a philosopher. You make your way through life with fearlessness and tenacity, you impart wisdom to others, and you have a great imagination. You can be with the truest reflection of yourself, as you are able to bring your shadows into the light.

When the water element flows with ease within a person, they feel peaceful and trust deeply—in their bones. They are comfortable with both life and death. They have tremendous courage and can endure many hardships.

When the water element is out of balance in your life, however, you may find yourself fatigued, and may have issues around fertility or conception. You may have back pain or soreness, and/or a disease of the spine. You could also have joint, bone, or dental issues with the imbalance of the water element. You may also have hearing issues, urinary tract infections, incontinence, or kidney stones.

The adrenal glands, located just above the kidneys, are also related to the water element. Adrenal fatigue may result from a water imbalance. Are your adrenal glands tired and depleting your energy system? Do you feel like you are always on high alert? Does fear run as a constant recording in your life? In the natural world, being on high alert makes sense. Say we are living in a wild place, and we perceive a harmful threat—perhaps we are being stalked by a lion. The fear response stimulates the release of stress hormones, preparing us to flee and protect ourselves. This is known as the "fight or flight response." But when we are not running from a hungry lion and stress hormones are fueled by ongoing concerns such as a demanding boss, financial struggles, the return of an illness, or emotional interactions with an ex-spouse, these hormones float around in our bodies and can become toxic over time.

In our daily lives, we each pick the poison of the ongoing stressors we perceive as threats, and if we keep them plugged in, they can become permanent fixtures in our bodies. Slowly, our ability to find peace gets eroded. Our systems end up with a constant stimulation or hum—it's as if that lion is going to jump out of the bush and devour us at any moment. Over time, as a result of ongoing physical or emotional stress, we may experience adrenal fatigue. This can lead to symptoms of anxiety, exhaustion, or a weakened immune system that can then progress to a number of other physical conditions. This is how the emotional problems that arise from a water imbalance can create physical distress.

When you are emotionally out of balance, you may struggle with anxiety and may lack trust. You may have feelings of insecurity or feel overwhelmed, which can keep you from moving forward in life, like when water freezes, obstructing its natural flow.

I RECALL a fairly young gentleman in his late thirties who came to the clinic after he noticed some blood in his urine. I'll call him Jay. Jay had no urinary symptoms—no pain and no blood pressure issues. Jay was normally healthy, had no other medical problems, and took no medications. He enjoyed participating in extreme sports. He shared with me that he had recently run a double marathon, which he had completed. This is when he noticed the blood in his urine.

Jay's workup ended up being negative for any serious bladder or kidney issues, with the final diagnosis of exercise-induced hematuria (blood in the urine). The interesting piece of this puzzle is that I ended up seeing his wife (I'll call her Nadine), who came into the office with a broken toe. Nadine was also an extreme athlete. She still wanted to participate in a marathon for which she had registered, even though her toe was broken. I provided her with advice and education.

Seeing Jay and Nadine reminded me of a quote by author Amit Ray: "If you are driven by fear, anger or pride, nature will force you to compete. If you are guided by courage, awareness, tranquility and peace, nature will serve you." I could see how both Jay's and Nadine's bodies were taking the brunt of their extremeness. They were both addicted to extreme sports, in part, perhaps, driven by fear or pride. Neither Jay nor Nadine was ready to stop to look at what was happening with their emotional or spiritual health, let alone their physical bodies.

After seeing and treating them both, I saw one of their three children (I'll call her Bella). Bella was five years old and had broken her forearm bone while wrestling with her two brothers. She needed to see an Orthopedist that day. When I stopped to reflect on this family unit, I realized they were all drowning, with no lifeboat in sight. Jay and Nadine never stopped to allow themselves to feel what they were starving for in the realm of true nourishment. What they chose to participate in to nourish themselves was in part killing them.

The amount of harm or destruction that can occur over time can be devastating if we push our bodies in this way. When we live life on the extreme end of things, toxic stress hormones continue running rampant throughout our bodies. If we don't slow down and find new or different ways to replenish our systems with balance and peace, our system never truly heals. It's as if we are stretching our right arm up high overhead while attempting to find balance. When we walk through life in this awkward stance, leaving our left hand lost, dangling by our side, we are unable to take in what we need. As I stated previously, the left side of our bodies is the receptive side.

Usually, when things go sideways in our lives, we are completely unaware of how life became the way it did, and it is about this time that we trip and fall—literally or figuratively. A fall can be a wake-up call for us, though we have to choose to "answer the phone." If we continue to live disconnected from ourselves, seeking answers outside the self, we never find ways to nourish ourselves at the deepest levels of our beings.

AS NOTED EARLIER, the opening of the water element can occur with groaning. When you break a bone, for example, you groan fairly loudly, accompanied by the shedding of tears (if you allow them to flow). But once you accept the crack, you can start to heal.

The crack in our system is a necessary component for us to receive life's truest treasures. Your light will fill every cell of your being with love and understanding of how and what you need to truly nourish yourself. If the wonder and delight of life begins to fade, you may end up spending most of your time chasing something outside yourself. If you continue running through life, you may miss the opportunity to know what it feels like to enjoy the present moment, and to experience internal peace and happiness.

In the case of the family I treated, Nadine and Bella's broken bones symbolized a "crack in the system." It was as if Bella had no choice but to join in with the parents' extreme behavior. Perhaps, in an unconscious way, she tried to assist the family by providing another opportunity for them to heal. It truly was no accident that this family ended up the way they did. Jay pushed his body so far that he bled, his kidneys (water element) were taxed with the extreme amount of stress he had placed on his body. Nadine was disconnected from the nurturance of the earth and herself at that time, and was not able to fully plant down due to her broken toe. Bella, whose bone structure was still taking form, broke her arm, clearly illustrating the family lineage. Jay and Nadine were in a state of avoidance, searching for ways to satiate themselves, not realizing they were taking part in destroying what they had built.

REFLECTING on the symbolism of the water imbalance being displayed by this beautiful family at that juncture in their lives, I thought perhaps their situation was showing me one or more pieces of my own puzzle that I had yet to fully comprehend. How was my own body communicating with me?

When parts of our body start to speak to us, we have to slow down enough to make the conscious choice to understand its messages. When it comes to the element of water, if we stop to acknowledge what's below the surface, if we look at our true reflection, our awareness will bring us to deeper understandings of our beings. The question of how and when we get our spiritual lessons is up to us. We can choose to look at such events in life as lessons—or not. Many times, the funny universe will keep us on our toes by providing us yet another challenging person or situation—or perhaps another broken bone—if we don't get the message in the first go-around. All of these things are in part necessary to bring our attention back to ourselves once again.

I have had many profound conversations with people that I call "meetings of the soul." In those moments when truth is revealed, there is no judgment—just an expression of truth. It is up to us to do the work and take the time for self-reflection. This can bring about an enormous shift in the soul. Love does tell the truth all the way, meaning that when we are told the truth, we know it. Love does not waver from the truth, even though the truth can be hard to digest or difficult to handle. But once we start living in truth, it becomes impossible to live from our authentic self in any other way than from truth.

When we begin to walk the path of becoming our authentic selves, we need to accept all parts of ourselves, the light and the dark. We need to allow whatever is inside us to have a safe space, so it can come to the surface, so we can heal it. One of the most common issues I see with people are physical manifestations of emotional distress—specifically anxiety.

Anxiety seems to plague many people today, young and old alike. I previously spoke about the use of tapping (EFT), along with breathwork and grounding techniques. These are all ways to assist people having issues with anxiety. Sometimes, just taking some slow, deep breaths with someone allows them a moment of relief. Other times, just by being witnessed and feeling supported, one can feel safe enough to dissipate some anxiety. The use of prescription medications (and now, medical marijuana) has become a go-to treatment for many, which I recommend—when such medications are necessary and warranted. But many times, just staying with someone through whatever they are going through in that moment can help them open their emotional container. Just sitting calmly, being present for someone, can help them see that things may not be as scary as they perceive them to be. They may leave and find themselves not grabbing for something so quickly, for they find that they can trust themselves and their own systems. Learning to be still and in-the-moment with someone is worth the effort. Often, the outcome may turn out different than anticipated—sometimes being witnessed is enough to catalyze the body's own natural healing abilities. The truth is, in order to heal ourselves and assist others, we must begin to check in with ourselves and understand what a "calm system" looks and feels like within us.

I HAD a beautiful young massage therapist student (I'll call her Joan) come in to see me after falling and hitting her head. Joan had fainted when she was working on someone during her training. As she shared her information, I could feel a low-lying anxiety coming through her words, as she spoke. Her neurologic and cardiac exams and labs all checked out fine. I felt she probably had very little oxygen going to her brain before she fainted.

When Joan spoke, she rose up on her toes, like a ballerina. Most likely, she lived from an ungrounded place, and that didn't help with her anxiety. I had her sit in a chair, and I pulled my stool in front of her. We began by grounding-in. I had her plant her feet firmly on the floor and do some conscious breathing, taking in full, deep breaths, bringing herself and her body fully into the present. For Joan, it was as if this was not something *she* had been doing—she seemed unaware her body was even here on the earth. Sometimes I place my hands atop people's feet or step on them gently. This gives them a felt-sense of what it feels like to be on solid ground and helps them to plant into the earth.

Following the breathing and grounding exercises, I had Joan begin rubbing her adrenal/kidney area to begin to break up the "frozen" energy in her system. She began to then feel heat (energy) in the area. I use specific sounds to open these meridians, which can help to dissipate some of the anxiety. I don't usually introduce the sound aspect in an exam room, because often people are too embarrassed. However, in light of the goose egg on her forehead, and falling flat on her face, Joan was up for anything at this point. It was only a minute or two before she began to cry, opening and releasing some part of a holding she didn't understand. Most often, below feelings of anxiety there is a layer of sadness. Allowing that to open can release some of the anxiety. Like everything, it's a process and individual to each person, but I have found this technique to be successful with many people.

Later, when Joan was checking out at the front desk, she said, "I haven't felt this calm in, I don't know when!" Upon her return to the clinic a week later, she shared that her sister and friends couldn't believe her new state of peaceful calm, and they kept asking what she had done.

I know we are all different and that not all of us are open to this way of moving energy, nor do many of us want to look at these techniques as a means to assist in healing. However, if someone wants to find a different method (other than another pill) to heal, then we may discover that this energetic release technique is an effective way to be present with one another while uncovering parts of our holdings. It is another means of allowing just a little more of us to come forward.

There is a beautiful stanza written by my favorite Sufi poet, Rumi, that says, "Your thoughts are a veil on the face of the Moon. That

Moon is your heart, and those thoughts cover your heart. So, let them go, just let them fall into the water." It makes me think of the water element and letting go of our holdings. Why do we hang on for the length of time we do? Why do some people go left instead of right? Of course, one answer to these questions is "Because we are afraid."

Fear can grip many of us and as I stated earlier, we may have no idea what it's all about. To deal with the fear that keeps us out of balance with our water element, we can push ourselves even more deeply out of balance by choosing to introduce too much water…in the form of alcohol. But whatever we use to assuage, avoid, or drown our fears, eventually we discover that we have to face them if we want to grow. And when we do face our fears, we bring forth our whole self. As Joseph Campbell so nicely shares, "The cave you fear to enter holds the treasure you seek."

How I chose to avoid myself along the way was primarily with food and wine. Until I hit college, excess sweets and carbs were my primary nourishment. That extra piece of licorice, and the pint (or sometimes the ½ gallon) of ice cream were my avoidance vices of choice. Then, when the bag or carton was empty I would think, "How could that be? Where on earth did it go?"

Another avoidance tactic for me was to overextend myself. I did not understand what caring for myself meant. What I needed, and what I had to do to come into a state of balance, eluded me— somehow it was lost along the way. In order to heal from the inside out, I needed to re-learn how to nourish myself. I needed to take the advice I was handing out to others. It was time for me to take in and fully digest my own medicine. My medicine included a prescription of truth: a meeting of my soul, face-to-face, allowed all parts of me to come forward, including the parts I had avoided up until then (which included my own family lineage).

My mother never drank, nor did her parents. Yes, an Irish family without the drink! Of her seven siblings, only one drank any alcohol at all. My dad, on the other hand, was an only child, and he liked his beer. So, I came into the world knowing two ends of an extreme. Since I'm probably more than three-quarters laced with those Emerald-Isle genes, surprisingly, alcohol is not something my body does well processing. God knows I tried.

At that time in my life, I had yet to discover for myself what coming into a state of balance felt like and looked like, so I could fully digest my own medicine. At this time in my life, I was in love, in a relationship, enjoying life. I also realized it was just two months after my father had passed, and I had not taken the time out to grieve. I found myself joining in on those one-too-many glasses of wine. While at first it was for fun, in time it became a way for me to avoid my feelings. I was taking part in life, but I was forsaking myself. My time in the woods, my "me time," was becoming less and less. My weekly yoga classes were becoming almost nonexistent. I was losing touch with myself for the sake of another person. I was on yet another train that I never recalled boarding.

At that point in life, I was not providing myself the respite I needed. My nervous system had no time to catch a break. I ended up with insomnia. My routine became no alcohol the night before work, because I knew that my body really didn't process alcohol that well. I even stopped eating sugar, but my sleep issue continued. I checked my hormone levels, but found nothing amiss. Something was not quite right in my physical body. Up until this time, I'd thought I was so good at keeping myself in balance.

At that time, I was working in an Integrative medicine clinic. I was diagnosing a lot of people with Lyme disease. The physician I worked with would ask why I even tested certain people because she was not convinced they had it...but sure enough they tested positive for Lyme. I kept Mr. Einstein's theory in the forefront of my mind: *like attracts like.* I then decided to test myself and yes, that spirochete (the spiral-shaped Lyme bacteria) had decided to wake up in my system. I concluded that I'd had it for many years because I had been removing ticks off my body several years back, while living and working on Martha's Vineyard and spending summers on Cape Cod as a child. No one really knew how long I'd had it. I was also aware that this illness can lay dormant for many years and not become active until the body is under stress. All those years prior, I did a fairly good job of maintaining balance—occasionally a glass or two of wine with a rare night of going overboard with friends. I had also spent a great deal of time out in nature, ate well, and kept my body in check.

I began treating the Lyme disease and chose homeopathy, energy medicine, and exercise as my primary treatment plan. It was not fully healed, however, until I completely embodied the wisdom and medicine the elements held for me. One day, I was out hiking on a Miwok trail that I had been on many times before—a place with sacred landmarks along the trail. I was not paying attention, and I lost my footing and slipped as I was climbing up on a boulder. I did a nice full body face-plant directly onto my left cheek. I wasn't sure if my cheekbone was broken or if I had a bone bruise. I also sustained a significant laceration that needed sutures and emergency care. I had been an avid hiker and had never fallen from any height, let alone from a two-foot boulder. That fall shook up my entire nervous system. After healing from that, I could still feel something was out of balance in my system. The truth was, like that spirochete, my soul was also lying dormant. The laceration that ripped my skin (metal element) open informed me that my spirit was torn. I was disconnected from the wonder and delight of my truest nature, not in right relations with myself or the earth.

After some time, I realized my entire system needed to heal on all levels, so I chose to take a solo journey for two weeks to Ireland. I mapped out a journey to the sacred sites with my end point in County Mayo, the home of my ancestors. Over those two weeks of walking, I spent time taking in the energy of those that had walked before me, allowing my own ancestral baggage to release. I ended my journey at my grandmother's grave.

On my trek through Ireland, I understood what I had been avoiding until then. I hadn't felt that much peace in my system for quite some time. That constant hum I knew was in so many people, I also knew existed in me. It had probably been in my system for many years, although now it was obviously taking a toll on my physical body. My emotional garbage can was full and overflowing. I knew from my many years in emergency medicine that this had become a part of my way of being. I also understood that if I stayed on this path, holding on, that my system would not be able to stay strong for long.

As I made my way across Ireland, I also realized I was flushing out toxins—physical, emotional, and spiritual toxins—that I had accumulated over time. As I was walking, I was also taking in those nutrient-rich energies. My vision was becoming clear once again, as I honored the lands upon which I walked. I was allowing myself to be honored in a way I had forgotten. My bones were gathering these neutral frequencies of the earth; they cleansed my being on the deepest of levels. It was as if those ancestral bags were organically going back to the land for composting. It was part of the new language I was beginning to speak.

I was nearing the end of my trip, and I knew I was going to have to make some changes. Recalling when I had fallen on my face while out hiking on that land—land that was filled with many spiritual offerings—was a wakeup call, showing me how little respect I'd had for my own spirit, let alone those who had traveled before me. I also knew that it was now time to share with others what I had learned and had shared with only a few.

THE TRUTH of who we really are is one with source. Avoiding myself wasn't benefiting anyone, especially me. My deep, reflective nature is part of who I am. I was not allowing that part of me any time or space and that was, in part, killing off the truth of my own existence. I saw my true reflection in my own mirror—and I needed attention. It was my time to begin anew. The pattern that I needed to change required that I remove myself, so I could polish my own mirror. I needed to let go of my old, familiar self so that I could become my true, authentic self. I knew that once I took that step forward to embrace the new me, I could never go back. Author Azar Nafisi's words rung true for me, during that time of my journey: "You get a strange feeling when you're about to leave a place, like you'll not only miss the people you love, but you'll miss the person you are now at this time and this place, because you'll never be this way again."

8

Wood, a strength that develops from the deep roots it grows.

W OOD BECOMES stronger and more durable when it is allowed to grow wild and free in its perfect imperfection. Wood changes and grows over time, as do we. People who embody the wood element carry a pioneer archetype. They are determined and ambitious as they make their way in the world.

The wood element is located along the gallbladder and liver meridians, the areas that have to do with our detoxification system. The gallbladder stores bile from the liver, which assists us in digestion and absorbing fats from our food. The liver has many metabolic functions and can convert nutrients to substances for use elsewhere in the body. The liver can take away harmful substances, rendering them harmless before they are excreted from the body.

Wood is considered the element of motion and is also related to our ligaments and tendons. A Chinese proverb states: "no movement, no life." The wood element opens with shouting.

The Color of the Wood Element is
GREEN.

When the wood element is in balance, a person is committed, decisive, and dynamic. They have clarity and vision, and they take initiative. They are patient and kind and are able to truly forgive others. Like bamboo, they are flexible, with a strong root system. Supported by the shoots that surround them, they are able to move and bend easily in whatever weather might come their way.

When this element is imbalanced, a person may experience migraines, eye problems, or disturbances with balance or coordination. Tendon or ligament issues and difficulties with motion relate to this element imbalance. This imbalance may also be displayed in persons with back spasms or nerve issues.

When wood is out of balance, problems with the gallbladder and liver can occur, such as gallstones or hepatitis. A person with this imbalance can be impatient, arrogant, or may have issues with anger, becoming easily frustrated or holding onto resentments. They can be workaholics, a bit reckless at times, and may have an addictive personality.

Working with this element can be hard because some people have difficulty looking at their anger. Many times, our frustrations arise when we cannot find a way to assert ourselves. Small children and animals are the best examples of beings who express themselves in uninhibited ways. They enjoy the freedom to roam, move, and assert themselves, expressing all of their emotions, including anger, freely. Then, seconds later, they can move on to the next thing, without holding onto the past.

When we adults direct our anger at someone, however, there is a sense of aggression connected to it. This type of energy may linger in our body over time and, if it is not released, we may end up causing pain to ourselves and others. If we continue the stacking up of our emotional garbage, our backs or necks may become so tightly bound that we have trouble moving them.

Most often, below this stuck anger or frustration is a sadness that has yet to be acknowledged or released. It's as if we turn in on ourselves with this anger. As the Buddha said, "Holding onto anger is like grasping a hot coal with the intent of throwing it at someone else. You are the one who gets burnt." Being burnt is painful.

Holding onto anger doesn't enliven us, it deadens us. If we continue taking in and metabolizing this energy, it can end up being stored somewhere in our body and can cause physical challenges. These places within us that we stuff or avoid usually find a way back into our realities, in some shape or form, and get our attention— usually through discomfort or pain.

If we can't move due to injury or debilitating pain, we have to look for alternative ways to move the energy. If we allow ourselves to feel beneath the anger and frustration, for example, we can find another pathway of expression to avoid storing these emotions in our bodies. Movement is a great way to discharge these emotions. Yoga, Qigong, and Tai Chi are all beautiful forms of conscious movement to provide an opening in our emotional container, so we can release what we are holding onto. Conscious breathing too can assist you in getting behind your anger or pain, so you can get energy moving in your system.

Sometimes, breathwork alone can break up stagnant energy, allowing some movement in places where we have had difficulty moving it, either physically or emotionally. Then, if we add some shouting from that deep well in our belly, it can assist us in dissipating some of that stored energy further. Of course, shouting without projecting anger onto another is best. These are some of the pieces of what makes us whole. If we allow all of ourselves to be present, we allow all of ourselves to heal.

On the other hand, if we continue to avoid "the cave we fear to enter," we may never find that treasure we seek. For example, we may keep our anger at a family member at bay by chasing it down with "just one more" scotch. Or we might release it in rush hour traffic, berating a driver who mistakenly forgot to put on their blinker with a litany of obscenities. If you keep yourself distracted, numbed, or in constant motion, you can keep your anger at bay. Yet by doing this, you are avoiding the energy that is causing continued unrest in your body. Stillness may have trouble finding a place to reside within you. This still place is necessary to allow us to be present to what our spirit truly desires to find balance. When we are still, we can listen to what our bodies are telling us.

One day, I was in a cycling class and overheard someone ask a young man what his heart rate was, as his watch had a heart rate monitor. He said, "I'm a bit over—my rate is 199." This is an extremely fast heart rate for anyone, at any age. Soon afterward, the man stopped cycling. The person asked, "What's wrong?" He said, "I have a terrible muscle cramp," as he began massaging his calf. That message came from his body, telling him his heart rate was too fast. He'd kept peddling without paying attention, so his body spoke again with a muscle cramp.

Most of us can relate to this concept of pushing or overextending ourselves in some part of our lives. We have to slow down enough to hear or feel what nourishment our bodies truly need or desire. Often the physical signals get missed, especially when we choose not to listen. Our bodies are the vehicles that bring us to the many aspects of ourselves, even those that can remain somewhat hidden. If we don't slow down enough and pay attention to our body's messages, the signals will become louder and louder until we have no other option but to stop.

Some time ago, I saw a gentleman in his early sixties while in clinic. I'll call him Jim. At first glance, Jim appeared to be outwardly fit. He was having intermittent bouts of abdominal pain. He had a history of Hepatitis B, a liver problem. I figured that Jim's body had been shouting to get his attention for a while, but he had chosen not to listen. I asked him if he had an issue with alcohol—something that could aggravate his hepatitis. Jim said, "It's under control, and I only drink once in a while, but most recently, yes, I have been drinking...I guess now is my 'once in a while.'"

When I asked Jim more about his life, he shared that he was currently in an anger management class due to his behavior at work. He held a supervisory position and had twenty staff members, mostly women. He was short with his staff, abrupt, and his frustration with everyone and everything around him was notable. Eight years prior, he had gone through a painful divorce with no amicable resolution.

After receiving results from his lab work, I checked back with Jim. I could see the pain he was carrying. It was as if he had a wall around him and no one was allowed to come close. Like many people, Jim was not open to accepting even the slightest suggestion to assist him, as there was no "crack in his system" to allow anything or anyone in. It was probably an unresolved issue that had been festering beneath the surface of his life for years.

Jim needed someone to accept him right where he was, in that moment of time. Meeting him in this place, seeing him for who he was, was the start of building a relationship of trust and support. Clearly, Jim was projecting his pain onto others, his anger was the amount of pain he held inside himself. It didn't justify any of his behavior, but if we can be with someone without judgment, the benefits will be far greater than anything else we could offer in those moments. Mark Twain once said that "Anger is an acid that can do more harm to the vessel in which it is stored than to anything on which it is poured."

Of course, Jim was "only hurting himself" with his anger—it manifested in his abdominal pain and liver disease—but his first step to healing was to shift that stuck energy by acknowledging the catalyst: the repressed emotions he was carrying. Were these emotions only from his painful divorce or perhaps from an earlier trauma or event(s), or was it a combination of both?

If our pent-up emotions don't move, it will be difficult to find peace so we can move forward with any sort of balance in life. So, if anger is part of our defense against pain and it is not looked at from its source, it's like having sludge in our gallbladder. This part of our detoxification pathway can become clogged and can create serious issues, if the congestion is not addressed.

WHATEVER the presenting complaint or stifled emotion under any one of the elements might be, there seems to be some degree of sadness below the surface. It's as if we bury parts of our emotional body when all the while they just want to be freed.

The liver is the organ that holds onto anger, the kidney stores fear, worry accumulates in the stomach, grief builds up in the lungs, and hate is held in the heart. I bring this to your attention because when we begin to balance the 5 Elements, that process calls for these parts of us to wake up. In those waking moments, if we can find a way to move these contained energies within our body, even in the smallest of ways, we can open our emotional container and free the stifled emotions we are holding onto.

Freeing ourselves of these emotional holdings is not about discovering the exact moment in time we started to contain these emotions or even when they became hidden. The reality is that we may have received many of these "buried pieces" from our ancestors. Accepting yourself, just as you are, right here, right now is key when taking our journey of self-awareness. Our perfect imperfections, and our many ways of being want to be acknowledged; they want to shift. Allowing ourselves to be present, instead of avoiding or running from the discomfort, may be what it takes to allow that bottled-up energy to move. In the end, the only way out of pain and discomfort to a place of health and peace is to go through it. Deepak Chopra's words resonate here: "Every time you are tempted to react in the same old way, ask if you want to be a prisoner of the past or a pioneer of the future."

RECENTLY, I was listening to a lecture, and the speaker shared a story about one of the oldest living Chinese men. On his 150th birthday, the man was asked how he kept himself going. He shared that he had a daily practice of meditation, walking, and Qigong, along with a diet rich in nutrients from the earth, with many herbs. These practices, along with keeping a quiet heart and never letting anyone steal his peace, were his secrets to living a long, meaningful life.

After hearing that story, I thought, "How often do we let people steal our peace?" If we don't find a way of making peace with ourselves and our stories, we miss out on bringing forth our innermost longings and desires. If we continually disregard ourselves and live life according to someone else's way, we lose the meaning and purpose of our own life. In order to be active participants in life, in order to discover what's next for us, we have to write our own book. By stopping long enough to take our own selves in, we discover the beauty our spirit wants us to embrace, so we can enjoy each chapter of our sojourn.

Many years ago, a friend forwarded me an article about the Hawaiian practice of Ho'oponopono (*ho-o-pono-pono*), a practice of reconciliation and forgiveness. It referenced a psychologist, Dr. Ihaleakala Hew Len, who was asked to work with criminally insane inmates in a locked unit of a Hawaiian prison facility. He accepted the job only if he could treat the inmates from the privacy of his office without the prisoners being present. Many psychiatric professionals on this unit had left this position in the past, and this was the only way he would accept the job. So, as he held an inmate's chart in his hand and looked through their file, he recited "I'm sorry. Please forgive me. Thank you. I love you." He kept repeating this phrase over and over. At first, he was taking in these words for himself. He began healing parts of himself that participated in the creation of each inmate's problem. He believed in the concept of taking total responsibility for one's life, wherever and however we end up. He accepted responsibility for his part in the plights of his patients. After Dr. Hew Len repeatedly recited this prayer, the management team began to see amazing results in the inmates.

The term *Ho'oponopono* means: *(ho'o)* to make, *(pono)* right—to make right with both the self and others. The practice of forgiveness can be difficult if we continue walking around holding on to anger. If anger is not spoken about or expressed, it will not dissipate—it will fester. Leaving these emotions unacknowledged or unexpressed will only result in them taking up residence somewhere in the body. We are all part of this larger ecosystem of wholeness, but if we do not want to remain stunted or stagnant, we have to engage. In order to heal, grow, and flourish, we have to connect to the heavens and the earth, as well as with the light and the dark within ourselves. Our hearts yearn for us to love all aspects of ourselves. Acknowledging anything less than our whole selves can limit us in being able to fully connect to all that is in this amazing and wonder-filled universe!

TO HELP others tap into their wholeness, I created a program called "Finding Your Inner Ninja." It was developed to assist our youth in discovering their own inner strength. I ask them to reflect on a place in the natural world or on a being from the animal kingdom that provides them with a feeling of unwavering strength.

I was working with a group of children who were dealing with cancer, and another group who were organ transplant recipients. Each child was partnered up with another child, with the objective being to find an object that connects them with their own inner power, while I witnessed and assisted them.

The expression of our truest self arises when we don't allow what is *not us* to hold space within us. When we begin to allow that felt sense of the truest version of ourselves to emerge while others are witnessing and supporting us, even in the midst of our pain and suffering, something can come forward and create a shift in us. When this felt strength surfaces, everything else falls away, even if only for a moment. Again, as Joseph Campbell says, it is ... "a very interesting shift of perspective, and that's all it is...joyful participation in the sorrows and everything changes."

I was honored to witness the inexplicable strength that emerged within each of these incredible children. This process also brought out a strength in me that I never knew existed. When we allow ourselves to be brought to these hidden areas within us, however briefly, we never know what amazing awakenings can transpire.

After each child had discovered their own "inner ninja," they created a picture and placed it in a casing to take with them as a keepsake, so they could have a touchstone that reminded them of who they really are. On the back of the picture they had inscribed what their ninja represented to them: "I am enough. I am strong. I am loved," and on and on. They awoke a part of themselves that was hidden and brought those parts forward to be fully embodied.

After our time together, I was gathering up my things and came upon a picture of a wolf in its casing. I set it aside. I was just about to leave when a young child came running towards me. It was his wolf. He'd come rushing back to retrieve it, as if he had left a part of himself behind. The hope and possibilities that were planted in his being—that only he fully understood—would now have a chance to take root and flourish.

FINDING one's truest strength means embodying something far greater, something that outweighs anything we could ever imagine in words or form. It's that something that lies deep within each of us that arises when we are acknowledged and fully connected to the well deep within us. That place is filled with unwavering strength. When we stop, when we provide time and space to acknowledge ourselves fully, we can erase any thoughts or feelings of insecurity, shame, or of not being enough. Then we find a strength that, when brought to the forefront, emerges far more powerfully than we could ever imagine.

I offer these examples of people reclaiming hidden parts of themselves, so that you can uncover and bring forth your own inner ninja—that place deep within that you may have been wrestling with. Your resistance, your holding back, does not reflect your inner strength or power. This is a projection that comes from your internal pain and lack of alignment with your connection to source. When you do not allow yourself to embody the unique imprint that you alone carry, it deprives our planet of the blessing of your whole, authentic self. Gaia, our earth, wants and needs you.

When I was pushing myself and my body, I knew on many levels what the cost of my own misalignment meant. I was missing an essential ingredient—stillness. Without finding the time to quiet my mind and my body, that place of stillness within me was never given space. This kept me from bringing peace and union into many aspects of my life. Being present and still allows your heart's compass to guide you with ease and grace to your best, limitless self. Today, I allow my body's wisdom to guide me back into balance—sometimes sitting quietly, sometimes taking a walk in the woods. On other days, I hike or do some yoga (and I still love biking, but I no longer have the need to push or pant to gain that certain body type). I am perfect with all my perfect imperfections, just as I am.

By uncovering the source of our own inner strength, rooted and supported in the earth and expanding to the heavens, we can access these places within us. When we are completely home in our body, mind, and spirit, connected from a place of stillness, we then have the ability to truly forgive ourselves and others—and that is a remedy that can profoundly heal the deepest parts of us.

9

Fire burns away what we are not, to allow our real self to emerge

$\mathcal{T}$he fire element brings with it a fierceness that can clear away everything in its path. Fire creates heat that can bring forth light—a light that can fill our entire system. A person who has a balanced fire element has an enthusiastic, transformative energy and can shine their brightest light to transcend separation, bringing unity to all. They are optimistic, empathetic, and intuitive.

The fire element is located along our heart and small intestine meridians. The small intestine's main function is the absorption of nutrients and minerals from food. The heart, in its central location, feeds our entire body through its major arteries, the vascular system, and the nervous system. The fire element also includes the heart's pericardium (a protective sac surrounding the heart) and the sex/ circulation systems, as well as the "triple warmer" meridians. The "triple warmer" includes the major organs of the pelvis, abdomen, and heart. The fire element opens with laughter.

The Color of the Fire Element is
RED.

When the fire element is balanced within us, we walk through life with a tender, compassionate, and joyous heart. We love without conditions, we can be passionately intimate, and we are creative, aware, and communicative. With a balanced fire element, life flows through us naturally and our entire ecosystem feels harmonious and peaceful, inside and out. Our mind is still, and our heart is open, beating quietly and steadily. As we walk through life, we can draw up the nutrients of the earth and take in the sun-kissed rays of heaven with an effortless exchange of love and joy. Perhaps Maria Marino wrote this wise phrase for someone with a balanced fire element: "When our hearts are filled with love and gratitude, joy naturally gushes out."

When the fire element is out of balance in us, diseases of the heart, such as high blood pressure, palpitations, or an irregular heart rhythm can manifest. Speech disturbances, sleep issues, anxiousness, restlessness, and an inability to feel settled in the body are common complaints of those who have an out of balance fire element. When fire is imbalanced, a person can be highly seductive and/or overly excitable. If someone constantly seeks out sex or drugs to sooth cravings of stimulation, or if they are beset by emotions of jealousy, rage, hate, and/ or greed, this could indicate an imbalanced fire element.

A DELIGHTFUL, forty-five-year-old Vietnamese gentleman I'll call Tuan, came into clinic with concerns about his blood pressure (BP). Tuan's BP had been running high on his previous visit, and we spoke about the possibility of starting a blood pressure medication if it remained elevated. Tuan wanted to try other avenues first, and he shared he recently added a daily blend of celery juice to his morning routine. His BP readings were in the normal range when taking his juice, but became elevated when he missed taking it. I also spoke to him about a concern, related to his father who had passed away in his mid-sixties from a heart attack back in Vietnam.

Tuan and his family were getting ready to go back to Vietnam for a month to visit relatives. We spoke about Tuan growing up in Vietnam and ended up speaking about the spiritual practices within his culture. The Vietnamese have a direct correlation to their ancestors and the natural world—where they find "God." Tuan explained that you pray to loved ones who have passed and give thanks to the elements (sun, moon, sky, water, and earth) and what they provide for you.

At this time, I had been working with a large Asian population, and learned how much of their cultural wisdom and traditions are part of their medicine. They utilize many medicinal plants and look to all that have come before them to assist when they are out of balance.

Tuan and I started to speak about his heart, his high blood pressure, and his upcoming trip. This exchange led me to share that his upcoming trip may prove beneficial in healing his heart on a level we cannot speak to (or many times, even see). He shared that indeed, there might be a place back home that he could ask his ancestors—as well as his descendants—to assist in the healing of his heart. His teenage son was also going on the trip, and Tuan shared his concern about what he might pass down to his son if he himself was not fully healed.

Tuan decided that he wanted to return to re-evaluate his BP readings on our next visit. He wanted to see what "medicine" he could gather on his trip. Tuan returned to clinic four weeks after his trip. Emotional, he shared his story about the extraordinary journey he had taken to his homeland. Tuan shared that it included time alone at his ancestors' burial sites. Tuan had started recording his BP readings again, and his readings were all in "normal" range, even on the days he forgot to take his juice!

Like Tuan, I believe that if we allow and hold it as a possibility, we can discover what medicine is best for our individual, unique systems. The interventions we in medicine provide to people can and do assist them, but if we remain open to other ways and means of healing, we may be surprised by what happens. I believe there are methods of healing that may not always be visible (perhaps orchestrated by Spirit or God), and that these can be potent and transformative, especially if we remain open to their potential. For example, we know that the healing power of prayer can be powerful—its power has been well documented. If you do not yet have a spiritual practice, I encourage you to explore the power of prayer and include it in your self-care toolkit.

When we begin to open to other possibilities on our path of healing, different options may start to appear and guide us to certain people, remedies, and/or places that can change the course of our journey. Once again, remember that not everyone can find healing from that "purple pill!" We are all unique with our individual vast terrains and landscapes. So, ask yourself: "What is the best way for me to heal?"

The experiences of love, joy, and creative expressions are all vital and play a significant role in the physiologic strength of our heart and vascular systems. If we begin to consider that loving, joyful, and creative experiences have an effect on our emotions and our circulation, we may embrace them as essential components in our self-care toolkit.

Of course, life is not always a bed of roses, filled with joyous, loving, healing experiences. It is also filled with trials and tribulations, and it is up to us whether or not we choose to address them. When our hearts break, for example, we can have devastating pain, but such events can also provide us with opportunities to heal. Similarly, if we don't allow ourselves to feel, express, or release what we have suppressed, our body's circuitry suffers. These emotional sources of ill health (along with lack of joy, love, and spiritual connectedness) can cause chest pains, high blood pressure, and many other physical ailments. All of these can impact our health just as much as (if not more than) life's ongoing stressors, our bad habits, our toxic environment, our poor nutrition, and our lack of movement.

THE IMPORTANCE of love and spiritual connection are beautifully drawn in this true story about someone who had come into clinic to see me. She was an elegant, Asian elder who had metastatic colon cancer. She came in with her daughter, who translated during our appointments. The mother (I'll call her May) had been seeing an acupuncturist for her pain control, but it was no longer working. Her daughter (Lily) was requesting a new pain medication and another scan for her mother.

While Lily spoke, I sat and held May's hand. Part of the heart's meridian runs through our hands. It was a way for me to be in genuine contact with May during the visit, as she spoke no English. I could see and feel May's beauty and essence as we sat together. The connection was one of pure spirit. There was no need to *do* anything, just *be*. I ended up giving May a prescription for a different type of pain medication to see if that would help ease her pain and enable her to continue with acupuncture. At Lily's request, I ordered another scan.

During our time together, I could feel Lily not wanting to lose her mother, and at the same time I could also feel May wanting to let go. I felt I was holding both worlds. I was providing a space of nurturance and support while being present and witnessing their love and pain— both very palpable during our time together. As I sat with May, she knew there was no language barrier between us, I was completely present with the depth of who she was at a soul level. I believe this is when our heart speaks louder than any language and can heal parts of us that are not seen on any scans.

I saw May three times, each time taking hold of her hand. On our third visit, May's spirit was so present, though her body was weakening. Lily shared that her mother wanted to come in to give me something. It was the Chinese New Year and May handed me a red, square note card. It had Chinese characters on it and a pouch with a

$5.00 bill enclosed. It was a blessing of luck that May wanted to gift me for my upcoming New Year...a blessing I will always cherish.

MOTHER TERESA once said that "Love is a fruit in season at all times, and within reach of every hand." It still touches me when I remember sitting with May, this lovely soul, knowing that my hand was holding her heart in a way, as she was preparing to end her time here. Being graced with the opportunity to hold another's heart in your hand is a privilege—a privilege I feel we take for granted sometimes. When we truly care for another, we do, indeed, care for our own selves.

This beautiful exchange allowed May and I to touch a place where our spirits were present with one another—perfect just as we are—right here, right now. When we remember who we are at the deepest level, when we connect with another person in this place, we can have an exchange where there is no illness. In that place, pure source and love collide. From that place, we can heal a part of ourselves we didn't know we needed to heal—until we do. The next time you are fortunate enough to be present with someone and take hold of their hand, remember: *this is a gift that far outweighs anything you will ever find wrapped up under a tree.* When you understand what your undivided presence and attention can bring to another individual, the exchange that happens within both your hearts reaches far beyond where spoken words can reach.

THE FIRE ELEMENT first arrived on my path while I was visiting my parents in Boston at my childhood home in the 1990's. I awoke in the middle of the night to what I thought at first was a burglary. I got up quickly to call 911 and then saw flames erupting on the porch. I switched from asking for the police to asking for the firemen. It was a three-alarm fire that ravished our entire home. My parents and I were out on the street, barefoot, in complete and utter shock.

I was blessed to have awoken after someone set our house ablaze. It burned to the ground. At this time, my parents were selling their home to a South African family with a skin color that was different from ours and those of our neighbors'. I mention this because an imbalance with the fire element means that the heart can hold the energy of hate—a strong, destructive emotion that I had no idea lived on the streets I played on as a child. An unspoken undercurrent of emotion resided in those hearts—so far from what peace or harmony felt or looked like. Many people in that neighborhood routinely attended Sunday mass. Was it possible that someone among them had been walking into church with a veil of hate over their hearts?

This fire in my parents' home occurred one year to the day after my ex-husband had died. This event carried something forward in me, unconsciously, that I had yet to heal. It was something I couldn't grasp or understand until I did.

PART OF the curriculum in my energy medicine training was to exchange healings with other students. It wasn't until almost ten years after that fire that I exchanged a healing with a beautiful woman of color—I will call her Diane.

As Diane walked into my home, she carried with her a bowl of ashes. It was an offering she'd brought for our time together, without knowing what had occurred all those years earlier. In that moment, my heart knew there was something coming forward that was important for me to heal. I knew that this was something that was well beyond us both, a gift we probably both chose to exchange on a deeper level of our beings. We were undoubtedly crossing paths at that time and place for a reason that eluded us both.

Diane anointed my forehead, my hands, and my feet with those ashes. That healing brought me deep into the core of my being. I knew, if perhaps only on a subconscious level, that some part of me, my lineage, was being healed from what had transpired in that arson so many years earlier. The roots of this exchange were a far greater gift than I or she could have ever anticipated. There was a hidden place within my ancestry (and possibly Diane's), that we chose to bring forward and heal at that moment in time.

The depth of what many of us carry needing to be healed within ourselves and within our lineage can bypass our conscious minds. I believe we are brought to people and places in order to transform and heal for the greatest good of all. This is the place of taking total responsibility for all of life. Like Dr. Hew Len, I believe it's up to us if we want to make that conscious choice to understand our part in the larger cosmos. To love in our truest form, we must let go of what we carry or hold, in order to allow our physical, emotional, and spiritual health to fully evolve and ultimately heal.

True healing can come about when we surrender to the flow of life and fully trust that we are all cared for at the deepest level of our beings. A heavy heart that carries the weight of hate, greed, or jealousy may never find its way to being set free. We must open ourselves wide and allow God's grace (or, if you prefer, "the light of the Universe") to enter us, to go beneath the surface to our deepest selves, and heal. As Dr. Martin Luther King, Jr. once said, "Darkness cannot drive out darkness; only light can do that. Hate cannot drive out hate: only love can do that."

Our ancestral roots may not be as clear or clean as we might think. Many times, we incarnate into this life with lives that have been tainted with strife, pain, and toxins, all of which may still reside in us without us ever knowing this is part of us. So often we don't know the cause of our disdain or heartaches as we go through life—could it be that the past life memories we carry subconsciously are affecting us on this physical and emotional plane? For example, I have noticed over the years that at the start of exams, when I take hold of people's hands, many of their hands are cold. This is an opening for me to bring up what they could be holding in their hearts. They can see and feel how their hands and arms connect up and cross their hearts. It's a way to start a conversation of acknowledging what their emotional container might be holding, a way to shine a light onto all parts of their being, and a way to access a deeper part of them that they can uncover, opening a new pathway of healing.

Usually, we are not comfortable speaking about these parts of ourselves, and these blocks are left to fester. I believe the universe brings us to certain people and situations in order to assist us—if we are open and want to truly heal. And sometimes, chance meetings can prevent someone from causing harm to themselves or others, by us just taking a few extra moments to acknowledge and support them. I can attest that I have been blessed many times to witness numerous occurrences of heart openings, just with the practice of taking hold of another person's hands. It's astonishing to me the number of young males I have seen in tears when speaking of what may be residing in their hearts. It feels so important today, with so many occurrences of mass violence and casualties happening in our world, to connect from this heartfelt place. When we do, we balance the fire element and bring true healing into the world.

IN OCTOBER 2017, the element of fire again found its way onto my path. I lost everything in the Northern California fires. The unrelenting flames that swept through our area took people's lives, homes, and many amazing landscapes. I was renting a home in Glen Ellen on an amazing spot that sat on thirteen acres of land and looked out onto the Mayacamas mountain range. I watched as a red wall of fire, spurred on by hurricane force winds, marched the flames forward at record speeds. My heart tore wide open, and it left me shaken to my core.

I chose this time of devastation and destruction to reflect upon what this fire element provided for my body, mind, and spirit. And I realized that each fire element experience I have had in this lifetime has always brought me closer to the truth of who I am. I know that it's all part of the process of making me whole. I also realize that as we grow and change and become who we were meant to be, the world we take part in changes along with us. Change isn't always easy, but to heal, we have to change. Life is change.

The Buddhists have a teaching known as *impermanence*, which is the knowing that we humans are constantly becoming and forever changing moment-to-moment. Just as the natural world embraces the never-ending process of birthing and dying, over and over, the key is to live our lives with no attachments to the permanence or impermanence of life. I have come across this lesson so many times, and I know that now is the time for me to fully embrace this teaching.

The California wildfires took my home. Initially, I didn't see the fires as a gift. But then I realized they were just that. I chose to see it as an opportunity for me to allow something new to arise. So, I believe I was given a blessing, or another anointing, from the ashes of my home. Like you, I am *forever changing, birthing, and dying over and over*, and every event in life can bring us to deeper parts of ourselves to heal. This book was another gift from the fire, *for this book actually wrote me* during this time of healing.

If we choose to take the deep dive into our body, mind, and spirit, we may begin to unravel where the disharmony, illness, or disease "may" manifest, instead of waiting until "when" it manifests. When life presents us with challenging experiences, we may want to ponder our choices. By listening and tuning into our body and spirit, we can allow our truth to be revealed to us. It is in this truth that we can begin to discover where we are missing out on what truly nourishes us on every level of our being. My hope is that you find time to plant thoughts that consist solely of seeds filled with love and compassion for yourself. Accepting yourself fully as you make your way on your journey makes the process of life that much easier. As a case in point, the story below shares what really matters in life: self-acceptance.

ONE DAY when I was leaving a building, a beautiful young woman asked me, "Could you do me a favor?" I said, "Sure, what do you need?" "How do I look?" she asked. "I am going on a first date right now for coffee and have no fresh makeup to put on." I looked at her and said, "Do you really want me to answer that?" She said, "Yes, truthfully." I placed my hand above her heart and said, "If the person you are meeting doesn't see this, you probably don't want to be with them." Her eyes welled up, and she couldn't speak. She placed her palms together and gently bowed her head in gratitude. Remember, no one can provide you your inner beauty or light. It already exists within you and yearns to brightly shine for all to see! Sometimes, we just need a little reminder now and again.

10

Coming Home – "Cead Mile Failte"

*C*EAD MILE FAILTE is a Gaelic saying which means *a hundred thousand welcomes.* When we finally come home to ourselves—home to our body, mind, and spirit—when we are living without separation, we come home to a heart that is in direct resonance with the energy of "Yes!" where all manifestation flows.

I completed a journey of many steps on the Camino de Santiago (also known as "the Camino" or simply "the Way"), a pilgrimage I began in St. Jean Pied de Port, France, to where I ended in Finisterre, Spain. When I entered Finisterre, I was greeted with a rainbow—a magnificent swatch of colors alive with a life-affirming glow—with the ocean as its backdrop.

It was a healing journey, 830 miles across mountains and meadows, woven with a tapestry of lush color—earth, metal, water, and wood were my heart's medicine along the Camino. As I started out my walk each morning, I would ask, "What color is my medicine today?" So, being greeted with this palette of extraordinary color as I completed my journey was a welcoming affirmation. It was an affirmation of taking part in the richness of a spirit-filled life, brimming with the beauty and magic that had been scattered throughout each mile of my walk.

The color of our medicine is unique and individual to each of us. We are indeed complex beings. By stopping, by sitting with all our complexities, we can bring more peace and clarity to our hearts and into our homes. If we listen, if we remain open to the signs, symbols, and messages that are all around us in the natural world, our hearts can guide us.

Embracing the wonders of nature can help us to discover how to release the inner holdings that have kept us walled off from our true selves. The inner walls we have built keep us from connecting to our self and source. If we allow ourselves a respite in the stillness of nature, we can reset. By engaging with the natural world, we can simplify, even for a moment, and find a way to live with less struggle, to fully embody that quiet space where our divine spark dwells. This is the place that opens our hearts to the energy of "Yes!" This is the place where we align and say, "Yes to it all!" Then we can invite in whichever color medicine will assist us in healing on the deepest of levels.

I RECALL a fellow pilgrim whom I ran into on and off throughout my journey across Spain. He was a gentle, sixty-year-old soul from Brazil. We saw one another many times along the Camino, although we never really spoke until the end, in Finisterre. There, he shared why he was walking the Camino. As a boy, he had been adopted. He never knew his birth name—perhaps he had led a life with a void he couldn't fill. He had never spoken of it, he said, until he started looking for a deeper meaning to his life. Just before his walk, he had learned his birth name and discovered that his biological parents had passed. Upon entering Santiago, the place where each pilgrim's walk is commemorated, it was here that he acknowledged his given name. He placed his adopted name, together with his birth name, on his placard. He shared his birth name aloud with me. As we teared up, he shared as if he had finally made his way back home to himself, whole for the first time.

That moment remains etched in my heart. Each of us is so unique and different. We travel on this journey of life—yearning to arrive home to ourselves. I saw myself in him, and him in me—a perfect reflection of truth. That feeling of oneness is the state of being that lives within us—without any walls of separation from anyone or anything. A poignant marking for us both, it was both an ending and a beginning—the end of a walk and the beginning of finding the truth of what being home with oneself truly means.

The name *Finisterre* (like that of the region of Finistère in Brittany, France) is derived from the Latin words *finis terrae*, meaning "end of the earth." "The end," can mean the outermost region of a place, and it can mean the destruction of something. In the latter context, our planet, Earth, no matter when or where we stand upon her, is always dying and rebirthing herself. She is never stagnant, never still, always fluid in motion, just as we are. She is ever-changing and when we engage with her, when we rest, get quiet, and listen, we are home.

AFTER LOSING everything in those recent fires, I know now more than ever that wherever I find myself, home is not about the house in which I dwell. It's about the home within myself. Saying "Yes!" to life means saying yes to *everything* in life. Life presents us life just as it is, with all the parts of the whole. The dark, the light, the yin, the yang—along with the heavens and the earth— all fit nicely together to make us whole. We choose what baggage we wish to carry. As we move closer and closer to home, the earth brings us its life-affirming energy. If we choose to treat her with love and respect, that is, in part, how we choose to treat ourselves. Do not forget, we are all part of the same system.

AFTER THOSE fires swept across the land I had lived on, all that remained was an angel outside my front door and a statue of St. Francis, standing watch over the property. Those figures, along with our pumpkin patch, remained intact. This was a testament to spirit's strength and presence in our lives. As we make our way through some of the most difficult times of our lives, there is something greater supporting us.

At that challenging time, many beautiful souls came forward to help in ways I could have never imagined. An enormous amount of love, compassion, and support came from many people I knew, as well as from strangers. They displayed their generosity in so many ways, it often brought me to tears. I was deeply touched (and still am today, when I remember each person who came forward with a word, a card, a hug, or a smile, on and on it went). Like so many people affected by the fires, I kept working, keeping myself occupied while doing what I do best. There was a baby girl (Rose) who came into the world during that time, whom I sat and visited with many times throughout my shift. Just sitting with that newborn and her mother was so healing for me. She gave me that pure love that babies come in with, and I drank it in while the fires continued to rage.

I began to understand what it meant to truly receive from the deeper crevices of my being. Out of a new language of the unspoken came the knowing that I am loved on the deepest of levels—as are you! The fires that swept across our area marked a time of initiation, a time of deep clearing and profound transformation for me and for thousands of others. For myself, I was able to let go, to walk across that threshold and through that door and say "Yes" to life. It was as if my left hand didn't understand what it was supposed to do until my right hand met it. It was a time of self-discovery. And I rose from the ashes, grounded, aligned—and whole.

Acknowledging and being present with our spirit enables us to acknowledge our potential for wholeness. Living and breathing all that comes to us when we choose to let enough go, frees us from our conscious and unconscious holdings, and frees us from any attachments to people or things outside of ourselves. By letting go of attachments to what might have been, our hearts can be freshly nourished by life's vast array of goodness. If we don't heal the past, we never step fully into our future.

After the fires, I found myself gifted time in Bodega Bay to wash off the soot and take in the fresh oceanic air. The element of water, the color of my medicine during those days, surrounded me with a fog and sweet mist. It reminded me of the sounds and smells of the Emerald Isle—they are such a big part of who I am.

I had a significant dream while I was in Bodega Bay—I was writing music with another person I know in waking life as a teacher of yoga and meditation. As my soul's music began to come into my consciousness, the magic and flow of life came back, clearer than I could have ever imagined. We are all artists, and each of these elements has a way of opening and expanding us to whatever tapestry we wish to weave. Whether it be through music, laughter, movement, shouting from the rooftops, or groaning from behind closed doors—all healing is welcome on the land, in the woods, by the sea, and with all creatures great and small. You are taking part in your soul waking up!

The body finds new pathways to healing at various times and season of our lives. Communicating with the color of our heart's medicine can take us to places we never knew existed. The fastest way to heal even some of the most serious of illnesses is by being open to receive, accepting ourselves as instruments of love and spirit. In that place within, we can find peace in whatever state we may find ourselves.

So, if you find yourself walking upon our dear Gaia, and breathing in her deep, pungent smells in a forest full of Wood, allow her medicine to make her way into you. Life can be muddy at times, but if we stop to weep upon the Earth, her mothering ways may nourish us. On other days, we may find ourselves beaming with joy in our hearts as we dance in the rain—all the while allowing the waters to purify us in places we didn't realize needed to be cleansed. Remember to embrace your diamond in the purest of form, that precious metal that shines bright for all to see and heals at the deepest level of your being. May you tap into the perfect, unending well of love and compassion that resides in your precious heart—and may your discovery free your soul and set it on fire!

Accepting where you are on your path assists you in accepting all aspects of yourself, especially when seeking change. For example, perhaps you wish to improve on a difficult health issue. Take some time outside, even if only for a moment, to breathe in fresh oxygenated air. Let it run through your entire system. In that moment, you can begin to set aside your health issues and create a new space of possibility to come forward.

Each of us is on our own journey, each of us attempting to find a state of balance and harmony. When we open to deeper parts of ourselves, we can take in more of life. Did you ever think that the person you find yourself in front of right now may be there solely for your soul's benefit? Perhaps, in any given moment, we are not there to fix anything or anyone, but maybe just to witness that person in front of us without judgment. By reflecting back to them our best, whole self, we allow them to uncover their own spark of wholeness. We are all students and teachers alike—and if our divine spark can ignite another's along the way, fantastic! Even during the most difficult times, if we allow a glimmer of hope to penetrate our beings, we may discover just a little more of ourselves and open up to something we may have never thought possible. The universe is awaiting the arrival of YOU!

I wanted to share with you this poem that came through me after a beautiful heart-opening, during a workshop I offered on the elements.

Woman of the Earth

I am a Woman of the Earth, I AM.
I am home now with my entire beingness.

I am opening, becoming,
unraveling into a woman of spirit ~ of change ~ of growth.

Bringing others together ~ Young, old, little, big ~
to awaken and unravel their spirits into beingness.

Taking others on a journey of the soul, on and with the Earth.
The natural world awaits our return ~

She awaits my return ~
To compost us, to awaken us, to live us and Be.

I am a Woman of the Earth,
who walks for the sake of the whole, in and with spirit ~

When I care for myself, I care for the Mother.
When I am aligned and balanced, I am whole, I AM home.

Thank you for joining me on this adventure into the elements. I hope you are able to find opportunities to sprinkle color and meaning into your medicine! May you always be open and guided to places and people that reflect back to you your true essence. Remember—when you live more fully connected to yourself and to our dear Gaia, she reciprocates. May you be ever more alive, and may you come home to your magnificent self.

Blessings to all on this journey,

— Regina

General Recommendations

This section features additional information on the 5 Elements, which can help you understand how to use the benefits of the Elements to improve your life and wellbeing.

Let us begin. Imagine waking up each morning, rising, and opening your closet door. Now ask, *"What Color is My Medicine"* today? This is a way to practice and play with your medicine each day as you're getting dressed. When you first open your closet, what is the color of the first garment you were drawn to? That is your medicine. Your body knows intuitively what it wants and needs to bring itself into a balanced state. Try it! Red shoes, green top, black hat—you may discover something you didn't know you needed, until you do.

You can also choose a specific *color* of clothing while holding an intention to assist you for an event you have that day. For example, you may choose a *blue shirt*—if you have a speech to give and feel anxious about it. Your intention with wearing *blue* is that you will open and balance your *water element*, helping to dissipate any fear that comes up for you, and help calm your system. Maybe you will wear *yellow* to bring in the *earth element* for a meeting with someone you have trouble holding healthy boundaries with and to help keep you centered and grounded. You may choose *yellow* undergarments if *yellow* is not your *color*! So, choose your color, set your intention, and let it go! No need to grasp, allow the universe to do its magic!

When your systems start to come back into balance, change occurs on many levels. For example, as you begin to vibrate at a healthier level, you may discover new cravings and desires for certain types of food. A clean body and clear mind work best with foods that are alive, unprocessed, and not loaded with sugar or an overload of carbohydrates. You may also notice that the environments in which you live and work no longer resonate, or that certain relationships are no longer tolerable. The less toxic you become internally, the more you desire to match that same frequency in your external world. These are all signs that your system is returning to its higher state of resonance.

As you come into balance, you may also discover your internal and external terrain are then supported by the Law of Attraction (also known as The Spiritual Law of Attraction). These laws hold that "like attracts like." When your true, higher self is in alignment with the divine order of the larger cosmos, you begin to participate purposefully in life. With your newfound health and balance, your thoughts, emotions, and body begin to shift and change, confirming that your vibration is rising. People and opportunities that can bring positive change into your life present themselves to you effortlessly, and you discover more aspects of yourself to heal. Your spiritual lessons become part of your everyday life. You begin to trust and surrender to the greater universal landscape and look to the universe as your ally—a friend that fully supports and assists you as you make your way through life.

Notice that every element builds upon starting with a solid foundation—grounding yourself into the earth. So, grounding as you begin any practice is a critical part of getting more in touch with your physical body. This can assist you to handle more of what comes out of your emotional container as you begin to open and release. Grounding, along with conscious breathwork, brings your whole self into the present. I highly recommend grounding exercises prior to beginning any practice.

TRACING MERIDIANS

Tracing Meridians can be another powerful tool to bring more balance to your system. I have used a beautiful YouTube video called, "Tracing Meridians with Affirmations" by Prune Harris. While you're following along, I invite you to pay attention to how you respond to certain meridians or how you react when you are speaking the specific affirmations aloud. You may experience a shift—whether comfortable or uncomfortable—that could reveal a place within you that is ready to heal.

OTHER HEALING MODALITIES

Earlier, I mentioned healing modalities such as acupuncture, acupressure, and tapping (also called "EFT" or "Emotional Freedom Technique"), as well as Qigong, Tai Chi, and yoga practices. All of these systems work to assist us in engaging with the 5 Elements. They are all ways to strengthen us. They open our systems up, bringing our bodies, minds, and spirits into balance. As you may be working with individual elements at different times of your life, in the following pages I provide specific recommendations for each Element. I also provided a list of references for those readers who wish to work with the practices and understand the 5 Elements more deeply. Hopefully my recommendations will reveal to you some wonderful pathways and help you to navigate your life's journey with ease.

Recommendations for Opening the Elements

THE EARTH ELEMENT

EMOTIONS

Positive attributes (+) Compassion, Sympathy, Empathy
Negative (–) Worry, Obsession, Over-extending
Opens with Singing
~ *Color* is Yellow

MUSIC	Drumming or drum music can open this earth element quite well. Remember, singing opens the Earth Element, so music and dance can ground and connect us as well. Have some fun with it! Think about joining (or starting) a local drum or grounding circle.
GROUNDING STONES	Stones can feel different for everyone, so holding and trying them first, to see which feels right for you, is best. ~ Jasper ~ Smoky Quartz ~ Hematite (Grounding the body)
GROUNDING MORNING RITUAL	Begin by planting your feet on the floor as you get out of bed. While sitting, gently rest your hands on your legs, palm-side down. Breathe in. Ask the earth to support and nurture you as you connect into her root system, so that you can begin to root deeply into your body from the ground up. Placing your hands in the dirt or gardening connects you into earth's frequencies.

YOGA POSE	Warrior One opens your stomach meridian along the earth element. Also, doing wide stance squats can ground you into the earth. If you find your legs quivering when you are standing in a squat for a period of time, do not worry. The body is releasing energy stored in your muscles.
MARTIAL ARTS	The practices of Tai Chi, Karate, and Qigong all assist with grounding.
WALKING BAREFOOT	Walking barefoot in the sand at the beach or placing your bare feet on a patch of grass while sitting in a chair are wonderful methods of grounding. It's important to hold the intention of allowing the energy of the earth to come through the bottoms of your feet.

THE METAL ELEMENT

EMOTIONS

(+) Ability to Let Go, Calm
(–) Unprocessed Grief, Regrets, Guilt, Fear of Death
Opens with Crying, Deep Sighing
~ *Color* is White

APACHE TEARS STONE – Obsidian

Begin by carrying this stone around in your pocket. I suggest placing it on the right side (the "letting go" side) of your body. Ask the stone to assist you, hold the intention of releasing—and then let it go! No grasping or holding onto your intention, allow it the freedom to release.

MEDITATION

If you haven't yet tried this practice as part of quieting your mind, it may be time. Meditation is part of the metal element. Meditation practice can be found in a variety of forms. Find what works best for you! Here are some options: Transcendental Meditation, Mindfulness Meditation, or a walking meditation out in nature. Or download a meditation app on your mobile device or listen to an Inward Journey at lauriekeene.com—a free gift on her website.

BREATHWORK

Breathwork is an integral part of meditation practice. To begin slowing down the mind, sit comfortably and focus on your breath. There are many variations of Breathwork to choose from, including Yogic breathing, rapid-fire breathing, nose breathing, and relaxation breathing. There is also the simple breathing technique I shared earlier: 4-4-4. You can also use 5-5-5, or 8-8-8 if you choose. The key is to start from a grounded place as you begin. Take breath-breaks throughout your day!

EMOTIONAL RELEASE

I recommend the use of flower essences to support the emotional body. They can assist with many stored emotions. For a specific remedy directed to the type of challenge you are addressing, speak with someone who has an expertise in flower essences. You'll find these experts at your local health food store or healing center.

Flower essences can be effective in helping people with grief. Grief groups can also be beneficial to people, as in such groups, like-minded individuals support and nurture one another during the healing process. You might also want to find a good therapist in whatever modality resonates with you: Cognitive Behavioral Therapy, Somatic Release Work, Energy Medicine, and Core Energetics are all effective forms of therapy for depression and grief. Do some research and find which approach might be best for you. Then, interview the practitioner or therapist to ensure you resonate with them.

THE WATER ELEMENT

EMOTIONS

(+) Peace, Trust
(−) Anxiety, Fear
Opens with Groaning
~ *Color* is Deep Blue/ Black

CALMING STONES	Lepidolite and Blue Lace Agate
"HIDDEN MESSAGES IN WATER"	The work Dr. Masaru Emoto has done with human consciousness and water shows that human emotions affect the energetics of water. For example, if we send purposeful intentions to water, we can positively impact our lives. To try out this powerful healing method, tape a printed message on a glass of water.
	Your message might read: "Strength," "Love," "Passion," "I Am Enough," "Calm," or "Peace," etc. Messages like these change the molecular structure of the water and as you drink it, you take in these messages and draw that positive vibration into your energetic system.
SYSTEM CALMING PRACTICE	Place your left hand on the top of your head, palm facing down. Place your right palm across your forehead. Plant your feet firmly on the earth. Holding your hands in place, draw in calming, nurturing breaths from the earth.

While holding your hands in place, let go of any rising thoughts or anxious feelings, and allow them to flow down into the earth. Again, breathe in calm, nurturing energy from the earth and breathe out any thoughts or anxious feelings. Do this calming breathing for five or ten minutes—you choose!

NERVOUS SYSTEM RESET

Take a Device Time-Out. One hour before bed, disconnect from all your IT devices—No TV, iPhone, or computer. Make your bedroom an Electronic Free Zone. Completely darken your bedroom, turn off all lights, and let your nervous system settle and calm. You can consciously quiet your system and surroundings in order to relax and reset.

BACH RESCUE REMEDY

This Bach Flower remedy works well to soothe mild forms of anxiety. It comes in a spray, in drops, or as tablets or lozenges. It can sometimes provide assistance in situations that bring up an emotional trigger—like giving a speech, performing, or taking a flight.

THE WOOD ELEMENT

EMOTIONS

(+) Patience, Forgiveness
(–) Anger, Frustrations, Resentments
Opens with Shouting
~ *Color* is Green

MUSIC AND DANCE	Find something that gets your body moving and shaking. And, if it allows you to shout, even better!
CHOPPING WOOD	Working with Wood to create furniture or other forms of carpentry.
STONES	For balance and strength ~ Tiger's Eye
	For forgiveness and encouragement ~ Rhodonite
WALKING MEDITATION	Doing this form of meditation while you are out in Nature can help dissipate anger.
QIGONG	Movements in this practice can isolate and work specifically on the part of the body that causes you pain. (*Mingtong Gu, a Qigong master, offers a practice you can easily download on YouTube.)

YIN YOGA	A yoga practice that holds poses longer, primarily to stretch and get into the connective tissue in tendons and ligaments. Holding the breath for extended periods assists with both physical and emotional release.
TREE STAND	A Yoga posture specifically for aligning the wood element. The pose helps us to become straight, strong, and bright. This pose aligns your Hara (level of intentionality). When we do this pose, our emotional container frees up and enables us to root firmly into the earth and connects us to the heavens.
HO'OPONOPONO (ho-o-pono-pono)	A practice of forgiveness that uses the following statement: "I'm sorry. Please forgive me. Thank you. I love you." Begin with self-forgiveness. Then, over time, without holding any attachments to the outcome, bring forgiveness to another person.

THE FIRE ELEMENT

EMOTIONS

(+) Love, Joy, Passion
(-) Hate, Greed, Jealousy
Opens with Laughter
~ Color is Red

ROSE QUARTZ

Carrying or wearing rose quartz will assist you in healing and opening your heart.

JOY MEDITATION

Bring to your mind a thought or an image of someone or something that makes you smile—like a child, your pet, or a flower. Holding this image in your mind, consciously breathe, slowly, in and out. Then, visualize sending this healing breath into all your organs. You can do this breathing exercise with every organ in every element, starting and ending with your heart. To receive the blessings of taking in your whole self, place your hand upon your heart. Allow JOY to trickle into your system.

STANDING IN THE SUN	With your arms stretched overhead in the shape of a V, reach up to the heavens. Take in the Sun. Allow its energy to flow into your heart meridian. For three to five minutes a day, before you lather on sunscreen, take in a few slow, deep breaths. Sunscreen blocks out many of the sun's nutrients. This brief method of being in the sun is Dermatology approved! So before applying sunscreen, allow yourself a good dose of Vitamin D, up to ten to fifteen minutes a day if possible.
LAUGHTER	It is indeed the best medicine. A good belly laugh goes a long way!

5 ELEMENT WORKSHEET

As you begin building your life of balance and harmony, you can have some fun filling in the lines below to support each element. I have provided some examples to get you started. If nothing comes to you to put down yet, no worries. There is no need to rush, it's a lifelong process.

FIRE   What makes your heart smile?
                      (e.g. Spending time with horses)

EARTH   What relationships nourish me?
                      (e.g. My book club, my friends.)

METAL   How do I connect with spirit?
                      (e.g. Sitting in meditation for 15 minutes upon rising.)

WATER   What do I want to learn or teach?
                      (e.g. Become fluent in Spanish.)

WOOD   What gets you moving?
                      (e.g. Riding my bike to work.)

FIRE (Red)
Creativity, Passions, Joy

_____

_____

WOOD (Green)
Motion

_____

_____

EARTH (Yellow)
Nourishing Relationships

_____

_____

WATER (Blue)
Learning and Teaching

_____

_____

METAL (White)
Spirituality – Divine Inspiration

_____

_____

5 ELEMENTS

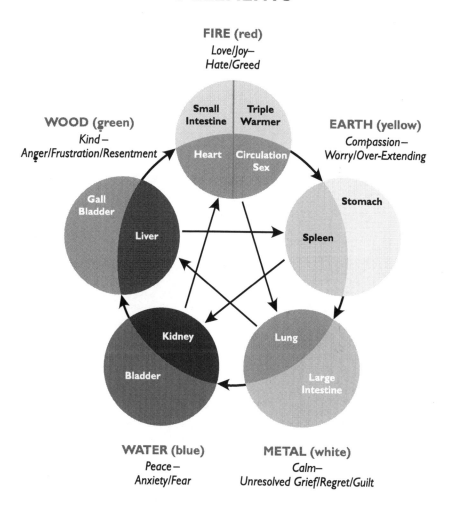

FIRE (red)
Love/Joy–
Hate/Greed

WOOD (green)
Kind –
Anger/Frustration/Resentment

EARTH (yellow)
Compassion –
Worry/Over-Extending

Small Intestine
Triple Warmer
Heart
Circulation Sex

Gall Bladder
Liver
Stomach
Spleen

Kidney
Lung
Bladder
Large Intestine

WATER (blue)
Peace –
Anxiety/Fear

METAL (white)
Calm–
Unresolved Grief/Regret/Guilt

NOTES

NOTES

WORKS CITED

Beinfield, H. and E. Korngold. *Between Heaven and Earth – A Guide to Chinese Medicine.* New York: Random House, 1992.

Brennan, Barbara Anne. *Hands of Light – A Guide to Healing Through the Human Energy Field.* New York: Bantam, 1987.

Chopra, Deepak. *Journey into Healing – Awakening the Wisdom Within You.* New York: Three Rivers Press, 1995.

Emoto, Masaru. *The Hidden Messages in Water.* Hillsboro: Beyond Words Publishing, 2005.

Gu, Mingtong. *Wisdom Healing Qigong: Cultivating Wisdom and Energy for Health, Healing and Happiness.* The Chi Center: Mingtong Gu, 2011.

Harris, Prune. YouTube video: "Tracing Meridians with Affirmations."

Johnson, Stephen. *Characterology Style.* New York: W.W. Norton & Company, 2004.

Northrup, Christiane. *Women's Bodies, Women's Wisdom.* New York: Bantam, 1994.

Rohr, Richard. *Richard Rohr's Daily Meditation: Christ is the Template for Creation.* Center for Action and Contemplation. Albuquerque: CAC Publishing, 2018.

Sweigart, Matthew. *Pathways of Qi – Exercises and Meditations to Guide You Through Your Body's Life Energy Channels.* Woodbury: Llewellyn Publications, 2016.

Thie, John and M. Thie. *Touch for Health – A Practical Guide to Natural Health with Acupressure Touch.* Camarillo: Devorss & Co., 2014.

REFERENCES

Academy of Comprehensive Integrative Medicine (ACIM)

- A place to gain information on the practice of functional medicine. A medical practice and treatments that focus on optimal functioning of the body. An integrative approach to health and healing—encompassing mind, body, and spirit.

Lyme Disease Information

- International Lyme and Associated Diseases: www.ILADS.org
- Byron White Formula – Herbal formulas used in the treatment of Lyme disease (*byronwhiteformulas.com*).
- If you have a tick for testing: www.tickreport.com
- Practitioners have been finding positive effects in the treatment of Lyme disease using Stevia leaf extract. For more information, Google *Lyme disease and Stevia*.

Sol Journeys

- A non-profit organization created to assist both young and old alike to come back in touch with themselves while reconnecting with the resonance of the earth's medicine. Sol Journeys offer journeys, retreats, classes, and workshops. www.soljourneys.com

Made in the USA
Lexington, KY
28 September 2018